Mediterranean Instant Omni Pro Air Fryer Oven Combo Cookbook

600-Day Fresh and Crispy Recipes for Healthy Mediterranean Meals to help you Lose Weight and Achieve a Healthy Lifestyle

Salia Cresp

Table of Contents

Introduction 5

Chapter 1: Basics of Mediterranean Diet 6

What Is the Mediterranean Diet? 6

The History of The Mediterranean Diet 6

Benefits of The Mediterranean Diet 7

Chapter 2: Basics of Instant Omni Air Fryer Oven Combo 9

Features of Instant Omni Air Fryer Oven Combo 9

How to Prepare a Meal in Omni Air Fryer Oven? 10

Cleaning and Maintenance 11

Chapter 3: Breakfast Recipes 12

Sweet Potato Muffins 12

Breakfast Kale Muffins 13

Veggie Egg Muffins 14

Breakfast Potatoes 15

Oatmeal Cake 16

Breakfast Cheese Frittata 17

Simple Cinnamon Baked Oatmeal 18

Berry Oatmeal 19

Crustless Quiche 20

Italian Breakfast Frittata 21

Mini Egg Muffins 22

Breakfast Oatmeal Cups 23

Mix Veggie Muffins 24

Chapter 4: Poultry Recipes 25

Lemon Garlic Chicken 25

Easy Chili Garlic Chicken Wings 26

Tasty Chicken & Rice 27

Easy Turkey Meatballs 28

Caribbean Chicken 29

Easy Chili Garlic Chicken Wings 30

Delicious Turkey Breast 31

Chicken Meatballs 32

Dijon Chicken 33

Chicken Casserole 34

Chicken Fajita Casserole 35

Tasty Chicken Tandoori 36

Juicy Spicy Chicken Wings 37

Chapter 5: Vegetarian Recipes 38

Cheesy Broccoli Casserole 38

Curried Cauliflower 39

Baby Potatoes 40

Mac & Cheese 41

Baked Vegetables 42

Potato Casserole 43

Spinach Bake 44

Arugula Artichoke Dip 45

Zucchini Patties 46

Delicious Potato Patties 47

Parmesan Hassel back Potatoes 48

Baked Egg Tomato 49

Veggie Tots 50

Chapter 6: Meat Recipes 51

Beef Chickpea Stew 51

Meatballs 52

Delicious Beef with Artichokes 53

Herb Butter Pork Chops 54

Cajun Pork Chops 55

Meatballs 56

Tender Pork Tenderloin 57

Garlic Rosemary Pork Chops 58

Garlic Pork Sirloin Roast 59
Paprika Pork Tenderloin 60
Oregano Lamb Chops 61
Easy Jerk Pork Butt 62
Burger Patties 63
Chapter 7: Seafood Recipes 64
Baked Tilapia 64
Lemon Garlic Tilapia 65
Sweet & Spicy Fish Fillets 66
Dijon Maple Salmon 67
Baked Lemon Cod 68
Air Fryer Salmon 69
Greek Fish 70
Tomato Basil Fish 71
Pesto Salmon 72
Chili Garlic Shrimp 73
Simple Salmon Patties 74
Chapter 8: Snacks & Appetizers 75
Spicy Almonds 75
Buffalo Chicken Dip 76
Tasty Zucchini Fritters 77
Easy Roasted Walnuts 78
Artichoke Dip 79
Cheese Dip 80
Ranch Chickpeas 81
Parmesan Potatoes 82
Creamy Zucchini Dip 83
Cauliflower Hummus 84
Sweet & Spicy Mixed Nuts 85
Easy Roasted Brussels Sprouts 86
Spicy Mix Nuts 87
Chapter 9: Dehydrated Recipes 88
Tasty Pineapple Chunks 88
Smoky Eggplant Bacon 89
Cinnamon Sweet Potato Chips 90
Dehydrated Banana Slices 91
Spicy Kale Chips 92
Easy Chicken Jerky 93
Dehydrated Avocado Slices 94
Dehydrated Strawberry Slices 95
Squash Chips 96
Dehydrated Bell Peppers 97
Simple Kale Chips 98
Dehydrated Shredded Carrots 99
Chapter 10: Desserts 100
Moist & Light Chocolate Cake 100
Delicious Peach Cobbler 101
Fudgy Cocoa Brownies 102
Blueberry Muffins 103
Baked Apple Slices 104
Easy Blueberry Cake 105
Moist French Yogurt Cake 106
Cinnamon Cranberry Muffins 107
Lemon Muffins 108
Delicious Strawberry Bars 109
Almond Butter Banana Brownies 110
Pumpkin Muffins 111
Conclusion 112

Introduction

The Mediterranean Instant Omni Pro Air Fryer Oven Combo Cookbook includes flavorful and easy-to-remember recipes. It will teach you how to make delicious recipes using the ingredients found in Mediterranean countries. You can cook by yourself instead of eating out, so you can save more time and money.

Including many recipes, The Cookbook presents affordable, traditional, and most importantly recognizable recipes to guide you on your weight loss journey. All of the ingredients can be found at discount grocery stores-nothing fancy here.

This cookbook includes many Mediterranean food in every recipe. Recipes are categorized based on ingredient type, so you will be able to find what you are looking for easily.

Chapter 1: Basics of Mediterranean Diet

What Is the Mediterranean Diet?

When studied historically the Mediterranean diet can be tied to a specific region or era. But scientifically proven the Mediterranean diet taken a much universally place in human history. Due to its unique approach to food consumption, it brings more balance to our diet and fills our plate with a healthy nutritional meal in a proportionate amount. It is an innate human need to consume food of all sorts, ranging from protein-rich meats to the fiber loaded vegetables, and fruits and the carb filled grains. So, this diet only works in light of such need. Its emphasis more on clean fats and healthy oils for daily consumption. The diet carried its name from its origin, which is rooted in the region around the Mediterranean Sea. People from those places were more reliant on seafood, fresh vegetables, fruits, olive oil, and whole grains. Their approach rightly guided the world to a nutrient-rich meal plan.

The greatest thing about the Mediterranean diet is it does not only guarantee good health, but it comes with so much flavor, aroma, and colors for our platters. Unlike, other restrictive diets, the Mediterranean diet is much more open and flexible. It suggests so many delectable options for every taste palate that it is easy for anyone to adopt. Over the course of time, the Mediterranean diet has significantly evolved according to different regions and culinary cultures. Today, it manages to prevent and cure several life-threatening diseases.

The History of The Mediterranean Diet

The Mediterranean diet that exists today originated from the stretches of Greece and Italy. Different classes of those societies individually contributed to the formation of this diet. There was a great inclination towards the eating of white omega rich meat including all seafood. Along with that, they use to consume lots of vegetables, fruits, and grains in some amount. The typical food patterns of the people in those areas were adopted readily by many due to the diversity of the nutrients the Mediterranean pyramid has provided. Over the years it existed as a culinary tradition, it was not until 1975 when American biologist Ansel keys and Margaret key collaborated to publicize the Mediterranean diet as a health-oriented meal plan. However, its widespread recognition came late in the 1990s. Studies regarding the benefits of this diet were conducted in Madrid and Naples; the objective data obtained revealed significant results. This study confirms the wide-ranging effects of the Mediterranean diet over people's health which were predicted decades ago. Later scientists came up with their different versions of the Mediterranean diet, but the one which was readily adopted was given by Walter Willet and his colleagues in mid-1990s. This approach was closest to the naturally evolved Mediterranean diet. It suggests a similar pattern of food intake as the people from ancient Greece did.

Benefits of The Mediterranean Diet

A healthy diet can do miracles no medicine can guarantee. Mediterranean diet is no less than miraculous if we acknowledge the great benefits it brings to human health. Besides accelerating the rate of metabolism and detoxifying the body from harmful oxidants, this diet can deal with a range of mental and physical ailments including cancer, cardiovascular disorders, and Parkinson, etc.

1. Prevent Alzheimer and Parkinson:

Both Parkinson and Alzheimer are neural disorders which result from the toxic build up in the brain and damage caused by it. The Mediterranean diet has shown unbelievable effects over the patients of Parkinson and Alzheimer, and they all experience improved mental functioning because of this diet plan.

2. Fights Against Cardiovascular Diseases:

All the cardiovascular diseases are linked with high blood cholesterol levels or weakening of the cardiac muscles. With the Mediterranean diet, such threats can be fought due to its good fat content. It does not allow the accumulation of bad fats and toxins in the body while keeping the metabolism active and running all the time.

3. Lowers Bad Cholesterol:

The olive oil based Mediterranean diet is free from all the saturated fats. Resultantly it is low on bad cholesterol. This form of cholesterol is responsible for blocking the blood vessels and causes a high blood cholesterol level.

4. High Life Expectancies:

Good diet and longevity have a very real connection. The better you eat, the healthier you stay. When you eat everything and balance, it can guarantee a long life. This fact is happened to be true for people consuming a Mediterranean diet, and therefore it is prescribed to everyone looking for higher life expectancy.

5. Aids Cancer Treatment:

Another curse of the current age is incurable cancer and the like diseases. Where most of the medicinal and chemical therapies fail to cure the disease, a change in diet have proven miraculous for most of the cancer patients. Mediterranean diet has been proven the most beneficial in this regard. People who are already consuming this diet shows about a sixty percent lesser tendency of developing cancer than the people who don't consume it.

Chapter 2: Basics of Instant Omni Air Fryer Oven Combo

Features of Instant Omni Air Fryer Oven Combo

As we know the Omni is a smart and multi-functional cooking appliance saves your kitchen countertop space by performing functions of the different appliance in a single one. These functions are pre-programmed so that you never worry about time and temperature settings. The front top display panel comes with these 9 smart functions and 2 cooking methods. These functions are

- **Air Fry:** This function is used to frying purpose, using this function you can fry a bowl of French fries within a tablespoon of oil. It makes your French fries crispy from outside and tender from inside.
- **Toast:** This function is used to toast your bread. You can put 6 slices of bread at a time into a middle rack your Instant Omni Air Fryer Oven Combo make it brown and crisp.
- **Bake:** You can use this to bake your favorite cake, cookies, brownies, muffins, and pizza. You can make a medium size (12 inches) pizza using this function.
- **Broil:** This function is used for browning the top portion of your desserts and casseroles. While using this function your oven produces dry heat from the top to cook your food.
- **Roast:** Roast function can be used to roast vegetables, meats, and your favorite foods. You can also roast a whole chicken at a time into Omni plus. In this function dry hot air covers your food from all sides to give you even cooking results.
- **Slow cook:** This function is used to cooks your food at low temperatures and also keeps your food warm. Due to lower temperature, it helps to preserve the nutritional values into your food.
- **Reheat:** Using this function you can reheat your leftover and frozen food it helps to crisp skin and retaining the moisture.

- **Proof:** During this function, halogen light is illuminated to keep your oven internal temperature warm it helps yeast for rising during the proofing process. It maintains 85° F to 95° F temperature during proof mode is on.
- **Dehydrate:** This function is used to dehydrate fruits and vegetables or meat slice for preserving. Making nuts and seed crispy, tempeh, crackers, oatmeal cookies, and drying your favorite fruits and vegetables.
- **Convect and Rotate:** These two are cooking methods. Convection and rotate are used to cook your favorite chicken with the help of rotisserie spit and forks.

How to Prepare a Meal in Omni Air Fryer Oven?

Cooking food into Omni is a faster and easy way to cook tasty and delicious food in a healthy cooking method. Following steps guides you to prepare fresh and healthy foods into your Instant Omni Air Fryer Oven Combo.

1. Prepare appliance by plug-in it into the power switch, the display light glows instantly then open the oven door and place crumb tray at the bottom notch of the oven. Always make sure that the oven is placed on a flat surface and leave at least 13 to 15 cm of space from all sides.
2. Choose the accessories as per the recipe needs and place them inside the oven at their correct position.
3. Preheat oven if needed, preheating oven saves your cooking time and also gives a nice texture to your food. Use your left side preset dial to select the appropriate program then adjust the time and temperature by using the right-side temp/time dial. You can also select cooking mode convection or rotate as per recipe requirements then finally press the start button. The preheating process is started the oven takes 4 to 5 minutes to get 400° F temperature.
4. After finishing the preheating process display indicates with a beep. Then insert the food into the oven and close the door. If you don't want to preheat the oven then just put your food into oven select cooking mode, adjust the desired time and temperature and press the start button to start the actual cooking process.
5. If the food requires turning or flipping then display indicates FLIP on screen. When you open the door to turn food than the current running program

automatically paused. After closing the door, you need to press the start button to resume the cooking process.

6. At the end of the cooking process successfully the oven will beep and your food is ready to serve.

Cleaning and Maintenance

After every use, you must clean your Instant pot Instant Omni Air Fryer Oven Combo to keep it germ-free. After finishing the cooking some food particles are stuck into the wall of the Instant Omni Air Fryer Oven Combo. Just follow the following some simple steps to clean your Instant Omni Air Fryer Oven Combo.

1. Before starting the cleaning, process unplug your Omni oven from the socket. Open the oven door and cool it down completely at room temperature.
2. Then remove all the accessories like dripping pan, steel rack, air fryer basket, rotisseries, etc.
3. All the accessories used in Instant Omni Air Fryer Oven Combo are dishwasher safe. You can easily wash it into the dishwasher and after that dry it completely.
4. Now clean your oven from inside by using a clean and damp cloth. Carefully clean all inner walls using a damp cloth.
5. After finishing inner cleaning clean your oven exterior body with another clean and little damp cloth. Clean display and touch buttons carefully with a soft cloth.
6. Now assemble all the removable parts like steel rack, dripping pan, and other accessories to its original position.
7. Check the power cable for any damage if it is damaged then change it in the authorized service center. If the power cable is ok then clean the cable with a dry cloth.

Now your instant pot Instant Omni Air Fryer Oven Combo is ready for next use.

Chapter 3: Breakfast Recipes

Sweet Potato Muffins

Preparation Time: 5 minutes

Cooking Time: 25 minutes

Serve: 12

Ingredients:

- 2 1/2 cups sweet potatoes, cooked and mashed
- 1 1/2 cups whole wheat flour
- 1/2 tsp vanilla
- 3/4 cup coconut milk
- 1 tsp ground cinnamon
- 3 tsp baking powder
- 1/2 cup coconut sugar
- Pinch of salt

Directions:

1. Line muffin tray with cupcake liners.
2. Add mashed sweet potatoes, vanilla, and coconut milk to the blender and blend until smooth.
3. In a large mixing bowl, mix flour, cinnamon, baking powder, coconut sugar, and salt.
4. Add sweet potato mixture and mix until well combined.
5. Spoon batter into the prepared muffin tray.
6. Select bake mode and set the omni to 350 F for 30 minutes once the oven beeps, place muffin tray into the oven.
7. Serve and enjoy.

Nutritional Value (Amount per Serving):

- Calories 134
- Fat 3.8 g
- Carbohydrates 23 g
- Sugar 0.7 g
- Protein 2.5 g
- Cholesterol 0 mg

Breakfast Kale Muffins

Preparation Time: 5 minutes

Cooking Time: 30 minutes

Serve: 8

Ingredients:

- 6 eggs
- 1 cup kale, chopped
- 1/2 cup milk
- 1/4 cup chives, chopped
- Pepper & salt, to taste

Directions:

1. Spray muffin pan with cooking spray and set aside.
2. Add all ingredients into the mixing bowl and whisk well.
3. Pour mixture into the prepared muffin pan.
4. Select bake mode and set the omni to 350 F for 30 minutes once the oven beeps, place muffin pan into the oven.
5. Serve and enjoy.

Nutritional Value (Amount per Serving):

- Calories 59
- Fat 3.6 g
- Carbohydrates 2 g
- Sugar 1 g
- Protein 5 g
- Cholesterol 124 mg

Veggie Egg Muffins

Preparation Time: 5 minutes

Cooking Time: 30 minutes

Serve: 12

Ingredients:

- 6 eggs, lightly beaten
- 2 potatoes, peeled and chopped
- 1/4 cup olive oil
- 1/2 bell pepper, chopped
- 1/2 cup green onion, chopped
- 1/4 tsp pepper
- Pinch of salt

Directions:

1. Spray a muffin tray with cooking spray and set aside.
2. Heat olive oil in a pan over medium-high heat.
3. Add potatoes to the pan and cook for 15 minutes.
4. In a bowl, whisk eggs with green onion, pepper, and salt.
5. Transfer potatoes in the egg mixture and stir well.
6. Pour egg mixture into the prepared muffin tray. Top with bell pepper.
7. Select bake mode and set the omni to 350 F for 15 minutes once the oven beeps, place muffin tray into the oven.
8. Serve and enjoy.

Nutritional Value (Amount per Serving):

- Calories 95
- Fat 6.5 g
- Carbohydrates 6.5 g
- Sugar 0.9 g
- Protein 3.5 g
- Cholesterol 82 mg

Breakfast Potatoes

Preparation Time: 5 minutes

Cooking Time: 35 minutes

Serve: 4

Ingredients:

- 2 lbs potatoes, scrubbed and cut into ½-inch cubes
- 1 tbsp olive oil
- 1/2 tsp paprika
- 1 tsp garlic powder
- Pepper
- Salt

Directions:

1. Place potato cubes on the parchment-lined cooking pan. Drizzle with oil and season with paprika, garlic powder, pepper, and salt. Toss well.
2. Select bake mode and set the omni to 425 F for 25 minutes once the oven beeps, place the cooking pan into the oven.
3. Toss potatoes and roast for 10-15 minutes more.
4. Allow cooling for 5-10 minutes.
5. Serve and enjoy.

Nutritional Value (Amount per Serving):

- Calories 190
- Fat 3.8 g
- Carbohydrates 36.3 g
- Sugar 2.8 g
- Protein 4 g
- Cholesterol 0 mg

Oatmeal Cake

Preparation Time: 5 minutes

Cooking Time: 25 minutes

Serve: 8

Ingredients:

- 2 eggs
- 1 cup oats
- 1 apple, peeled & chopped
- 1 tbsp butter
- 3 tbsp yogurt
- 1/2 tsp baking powder
- 1/2 tsp baking soda
- 1 tsp cinnamon
- 1 tsp vanilla
- 3 tbsps honey

Directions:

1. Add 3/4 cup oats and remaining ingredients into the blender and blend until smooth.
2. Add remaining oats and mix well.
3. Pour batter into the parchment-lined baking pan.
4. Select bake mode and set the omni to 350 F for 25 minutes once the oven beeps, place baking pan into the oven.
5. Slice and serve.

Nutritional Value (Amount per Serving):

- Calories 112
- Fat 3.3 g
- Carbohydrates 18.2 g
- Sugar 10 g
- Protein 3.2 g
- Cholesterol 45 mg

Breakfast Cheese Frittata

Preparation Time: 5 minutes

Cooking Time: 30 minutes

Serve: 6

Ingredients:

- 6 eggs
- 3/4 cup mozzarella cheese
- 1/4 cup fresh basil, chopped
- 1/2 cup tomatoes, chopped
- 2 tbsp water
- Pepper
- Salt

Directions:

1. Spray an 8-inch pie dish with cooking spray and set aside.
2. In a bowl, whisk eggs with water, 1/2 cheese, pepper, and salt.
3. Add remaining cheese, basil, and tomatoes and stir well.
4. Pour egg mixture into the prepared pie dish.
5. Select bake mode and set the omni to 350 F for 30 minutes once the oven beeps, place the pie dish into the oven.
6. Serve and enjoy.

Nutritional Value (Amount per Serving):

- Calories 76
- Fat 5 g
- Carbohydrates 1.1 g
- Sugar 0.7 g
- Protein 6.7 g
- Cholesterol 166 mg

Simple Cinnamon Baked Oatmeal

Preparation Time: 5 minutes

Cooking Time: 25 minutes

Serve: 6

Ingredients:

- 2 eggs, lightly beaten
- 1 1/4 cup milk
- 1/2 cup butter, melted
- 1 cup brown sugar
- 3 cups quick oats
- 1 tsp ground cinnamon
- 1 tsp vanilla
- 1 tbsp baking powder

Directions:

1. Spray an 8-inch baking dish with cooking spray.
2. In a bowl, whisk sugar, vanilla, cinnamon, baking powder, eggs, milk, and butter until well combined. Add oats and stir well.
3. Pour oat mixture into the prepared baking dish.
4. Select bake mode and set the omni to 350 F for 25 minutes once the oven beeps, place the baking dish into the oven.
5. Serve and enjoy.

Nutritional Value (Amount per Serving):

- Calories 434
- Fat 20.5 g
- Carbohydrates 55.6 g
- Sugar 26.4 g
- Protein 9.1 g
- Cholesterol 99 mg

Berry Oatmeal

Preparation Time: 5 minutes

Cooking Time: 20 minutes

Serve: 4

Ingredients:

- 1 egg
- 1/4 cup maple syrup
- 1 1/2 cups milk
- 1 1/2 tsp baking powder
- 2 cups old fashioned oats
- 1 cup blueberries
- 1/2 cup blackberries
- 1/2 cup strawberries, sliced
- 1/2 tsp salt

Directions:

1. Grease baking dish and set aside.
2. In a mixing bowl, mix together oats, salt, and baking powder.
3. Add vanilla, egg, maple syrup, and milk and stir well.
4. Add berries and stir well.
5. Pour mixture into the baking dish.
6. Select bake mode and set the omni to 375 F for 20 minutes once the oven beeps, place the baking dish into the oven.
7. Serve and enjoy.

Nutritional Value (Amount per Serving):

- Calories 461
- Fat 8.4 g
- Carbohydrates 80.7 g
- Sugar 23.4 g
- Protein 15 g
- Cholesterol 48 mg

Crustless Quiche

Preparation Time: 5 minutes

Cooking Time: 45 minutes

Serve: 6

Ingredients:

- 6 eggs
- 1 cup cheddar cheese, grated
- 1 cup tomatoes, chopped
- 1 cup milk
- Pepper
- Salt

Directions:

1. Spray an 8-inch pie dish with cooking spray and set aside.
2. In a bowl, whisk eggs with cheese, milk, pepper, and salt. Add tomatoes and stir well.
3. Pour egg mixture into the prepared pie dish.
4. Select bake mode and set the omni to 350 F for 45 minutes once the oven beeps, place the pie dish into the oven.
5. Serve and enjoy.

Nutritional Value (Amount per Serving):

- Calories 165
- Fat 11.5 g
- Carbohydrates 3.8 g
- Sugar 3.1 g
- Protein 11.8 g
- Cholesterol 187 mg

Italian Breakfast Frittata

Preparation Time: 5 minutes

Cooking Time: 30 minutes

Serve: 4

Ingredients:

- 8 eggs
- 2 zucchini, chopped and cooked
- 1 tbsp fresh parsley, chopped
- 3 tbsps parmesan cheese, grated
- Pepper & salt, to taste

Directions:

1. Grease baking dish and set aside.
2. In a mixing bowl, whisk eggs with pepper and salt.
3. Add parsley, cheese, and zucchini and stir well.
4. Pour egg mixture into the prepared baking dish.
5. Select bake mode and set the omni to 350 F for 30 minutes once the oven beeps, place the baking dish into the oven.
6. Serve and enjoy.

Nutritional Value (Amount per Serving):

- Calories 176
- Fat 11.2 g
- Carbohydrates 4.4 g
- Sugar 2.4 g
- Protein 15.7 g
- Cholesterol 335 mg

Mini Egg Muffins

Preparation Time: 5 minutes

Cooking Time: 20 minutes

Serve: 9

Ingredients:

- 4 eggs
- 1/4 cup Sun-dried tomatoes, chopped
- 1/2 cup Kale, chopped
- ½ cup egg whites
- Pepper & salt, to taste

Directions:

1. Spray muffin pan with cooking spray and set aside.
2. In a mixing bowl, whisk eggs and egg whites.
3. Add sun-dried tomatoes, kale, pepper, and salt and whisk well.
4. Pour egg mixture into the prepared muffin pan
5. Select bake mode and set the omni to 350 F for 20 minutes once the oven beeps, place muffin pan into the oven.
6. Serve and enjoy.

Nutritional Value (Amount per Serving):

- Calories 49
- Fat 2.1 g
- Carbohydrates 3.5 g
- Sugar 0.5 g
- Protein 4.3 g
- Cholesterol 73 mg

Breakfast Oatmeal Cups

Preparation Time: 5 minutes

Cooking Time: 30 minutes

Serve: 12

Ingredients:

- 3 cups old fashioned oats
- 1 1/2 cups unsweetened almond milk
- 1/2 tsp vanilla
- 1 1/2 tsp cinnamon
- 1 cup apples, chopped
- 1/4 cup maple syrup
- 1 1/4 cups unsweetened applesauce
- 1 tsp baking powder
- 1/4 tsp salt

Directions:

1. Spray a muffin tray with cooking spray.
2. Add all ingredients except for the apples in a large mixing bowl and mix until well combined.
3. Add apples and fold well.
4. Pour batter into the prepared muffin tray.
5. Select bake mode and set the omni to 350 F for 30 minutes once the oven beeps, place muffin tray into the oven.
6. Serve and enjoy.

Nutritional Value (Amount per Serving):

- Calories 200
- Fat 3.1 g
- Carbohydrates 37.4 g
- Sugar 9.5 g
- Protein 5.2 g
- Cholesterol 0 mg

Mix Veggie Muffins

Preparation Time: 5 minutes

Cooking Time: 22 minutes

Serve: 12

Ingredients:

- 12 large eggs
- 1/4 cup parmesan cheese, grated
- 1 cup cheddar cheese, shredded
- 3 tbsp onion, minced
- 1/2 tsp mustard powder
- 1/4 cup milk
- 1 tsp olive oil
- 3 cups mixed vegetables, chopped
- 1/2 tsp pepper
- 1/2 tsp salt

Directions:

1. Spray muffin pan with cooking spray and set aside.
2. Heat oil in a pan over medium heat.
3. Add mixed vegetables to the pan and sauté until tender.
4. Remove pan from heat and let it cool.
5. In a mixing bowl, whisk eggs, seasonings, and milk. Add sautéed vegetables, onion, and cheeses and whisk well.
6. Pour egg mixture into the prepared muffin pan
7. Select bake mode and set the omni to 350 F for 22 minutes once the oven beeps, place muffin pan into the oven.
8. Serve and enjoy.

Nutritional Value (Amount per Serving):

- Calories 146
- Fat 9.2 g
- Carbohydrates 5.5 g
- Sugar 0.8 g
- Protein 10.4 g
- Cholesterol 198 mg

Chapter 4: Poultry Recipes

Lemon Garlic Chicken

Preparation Time: 5 minutes

Cooking Time: 40 minutes

Serve: 4

Ingredients:

- 2 lbs chicken drumsticks
- 2 tbsp parsley, chopped
- 1 fresh lemon juice
- 8 garlic cloves, sliced
- 2 tbsp olive oil
- Pepper
- Salt

Directions:

1. Spray a cooking pan with cooking spray.
2. Place chicken on the cooking pan. Season chicken with pepper and salt.
3. Sprinkle the parsley and garlic over the chicken. Drizzle with lemon juice and olive oil.
4. Select bake mode and set the omni to 450 F for 40 minutes once the oven beeps, place the cooking pan into the oven.
5. Serve and enjoy.

Nutritional Value (Amount per Serving):

- Calories 456
- Fat 20.1 g
- Carbohydrates 2.4 g
- Sugar 0.3 g
- Protein 62.9 g
- Cholesterol 200 mg

Easy Chili Garlic Chicken Wings

Preparation Time: 5 minutes

Cooking Time: 20 minutes

Serve: 4

Ingredients:

- 12 chicken wings
- 1 tbsp chili powder
- 1/2 tbsp baking powder
- 1 tsp granulated garlic
- 1/2 tsp sea salt

Directions:

1. Add chicken wings into the large bowl and toss with remaining ingredients.
2. Transfer chicken wings into the air fryer basket.
3. Place air fryer basket into the oven and select air fry mode set omni to the 410 F for 20 minutes.
4. Serve and enjoy.

Nutritional Value (Amount per Serving):

- Calories 485
- Fat 18.9 g
- Carbohydrates 2.4 g
- Sugar 0.3 g
- Protein 72.7 g
- Cholesterol 223 mg

Tasty Chicken & Rice

Preparation Time: 5 minutes

Cooking Time: 1 hour 15 minutes

Serve: 4

Ingredients:

- 4 chicken breasts, skinless and boneless
- 1 cup of rice
- 14 oz chicken stock
- 1/4 cup butter, melted
- 1 tbsp lemon pepper seasoning
- 1/2 tsp salt

Directions:

1. Season chicken with lemon pepper seasoning from both the sides.
2. Pour melted butter into a baking pan.
3. Place chicken in pan and cover pan with foil.
4. Select bake mode and set the omni to 350 F for 30 minutes once the oven beeps, place baking pan into the oven. Turn chicken halfway through.
5. Remove chicken from pan and place it to a plate.
6. In the same baking pan stir together rice, stock, and salt and bake rice for 30 minutes.
7. Place baked chicken on top of rice.
8. Cover the pan again and bake for 15 minutes more.
9. Serve and enjoy.

Nutritional Value (Amount per Serving):

- Calories 545
- Fat 22.5 g
- Carbohydrates 38.3 g
- Sugar 0.4 g
- Protein 44.4 g
- Cholesterol 155 mg

Easy Turkey Meatballs

Preparation Time: 5 minutes

Cooking Time: 12 minutes

Serve: 4

Ingredients:

- 1 egg
- 2 tbsp coconut flour
- 1 lb ground turkey
- 1 garlic clove, minced
- 2 green onion, chopped
- 1/4 cup celery, chopped
- 1/4 cup carrots, grated
- Pepper
- Salt

Directions:

1. Spray air fryer basket with cooking spray.
2. Add all ingredients into the large bowl and mix until well combined.
3. Make small balls from the meat mixture and place it into the air fryer basket.
4. Place air fryer basket into the oven and select air fry mode set omni to the 400 F for 12 minutes. Turn halfway through.
5. Serve and enjoy.

Nutritional Value (Amount per Serving):

- Calories 274
- Fat 14.3 g
- Carbohydrates 6.8 g
- Sugar 0.7 g
- Protein 33.7 g
- Cholesterol 157 mg

Caribbean Chicken

Preparation Time: 5 minutes

Cooking Time: 10 minutes

Serve: 8

Ingredients:

- 3 lbs chicken thigh, skinless and boneless
- 1 tbsp cayenne
- 1 tbsp cinnamon
- 1 tbsp coriander powder
- 3 tbsp coconut oil, melted
- 1/2 tsp ground nutmeg
- 1/2 tsp ground ginger
- Pepper
- Salt

Directions:

1. In a small bowl, mix together all ingredients except chicken.
2. Rub bowl mixture all over the chicken.
3. Spray air fryer basket with cooking spray.
4. Place chicken into the air fryer basket.
5. Place air fryer basket into the oven and select air fry mode set omni to the 390 F for 10 minutes.
6. Serve and enjoy.

Nutritional Value (Amount per Serving):

- Calories 373
- Fat 17.9 g
- Carbohydrates 1.2 g
- Sugar 0.1 g
- Protein 49.3 g
- Cholesterol 151 mg

Easy Chili Garlic Chicken Wings

Preparation Time: 5 minutes

Cooking Time: 60 minutes

Serve: 4

Ingredients:

- 2 lbs chicken wings
- 1/8 tsp paprika
- 2 tsp seasoned salt
- 1/2 cup coconut flour
- 1/4 tsp garlic powder
- 1/4 tsp chili powder

Directions:

1. In a mixing bowl, add all ingredients except chicken wings and mix well.
2. Add chicken wings to the bowl and coat well and place it on a cooking pan.
3. Select bake mode and set the omni to 400 F for 60 minutes once the oven beeps, place the cooking pan into the oven.
4. Serve and enjoy.

Nutritional Value (Amount per Serving):

- Calories 492
- Fat 18.4 g
- Carbohydrates 10.3 g
- Sugar 0.1 g
- Protein 67.7 g
- Cholesterol 202 mg

Delicious Turkey Breast

Preparation Time: 5 minutes

Cooking Time: 45 minutes

Serve: 4

Ingredients:

- 1 lb turkey breast, cut into 1-inch cubes
- 1 tsp garlic powder
- 1/2 lb Brussels sprouts, cut in half
- 2 tbsp olive oil
- 1 cup mushrooms, cleaned
- Pepper
- Salt

Directions:

1. In a small bowl, mix oil, garlic powder, pepper, and salt.
2. In a baking dish, mix together turkey, mushrooms, and Brussels sprouts. Pour oil mixture on top.
3. Cover dish with foil. Select bake mode and set the omni to 350 F for 45 minutes once the oven beeps, place the baking dish into the oven.
4. Serve and enjoy.

Nutritional Value (Amount per Serving):

- Calories 209
- Fat 9.1 g
- Carbohydrates 11 g
- Sugar 5.7 g
- Protein 22 g
- Cholesterol 49 mg

Chicken Meatballs

Preparation Time: 5 minutes

Cooking Time: 10 minutes

Serve: 4

Ingredients:

- 1 lb ground chicken
- 1/4 cup shredded coconut
- 1 tsp sesame oil
- 1 tbsp hoisin sauce
- 1/2 cup fresh cilantro, chopped
- 2 green onions, chopped
- 1 tsp sriracha
- 1 tbsp soy sauce
- Pepper
- Salt

Directions:

1. Spray air fryer basket with cooking spray.
2. Add all ingredients into the large mixing bowl and mix until well combined.
3. Make small balls from bowl mixture and place it into the air fryer basket.
4. Place air fryer basket into the oven and select air fry mode set omni to the 350 F for 10 minutes. Turn halfway through.
5. Serve and enjoy.

Nutritional Value (Amount per Serving):

- Calories 258
- Fat 11.4 g
- Carbohydrates 3.7 g
- Sugar 1.7 g
- Protein 33.5 g
- Cholesterol 101 mg

Dijon Chicken

Preparation Time: 5 minutes

Cooking Time: 50 minutes

Serve: 4

Ingredients:

- 1 1/2 lbs chicken thighs, skinless and boneless
- 2 tbsp Dijon mustard
- 1/4 cup French mustard
- 4 tbsp maple syrup
- 2 tsp olive oil

Directions:

1. In a mixing bowl, mix together maple syrup, olive oil, Dijon mustard, and French mustard.
2. Add chicken to the bowl and mix until chicken is well coated with maple mixture.
3. Arrange chicken in a baking dish.
4. Select bake mode and set the omni to 375 F for 50 minutes once the oven beeps, place the baking dish into the oven.
5. Serve and enjoy.

Nutritional Value (Amount per Serving):

- Calories 401
- Fat 15.3 g
- Carbohydrates 13.8 g
- Sugar 12 g
- Protein 49.6 g
- Cholesterol 151 mg

Chicken Casserole

Preparation Time: 5 minutes

Cooking Time: 35 minutes

Serve: 8

Ingredients:

- 2 1/2 lbs chicken breasts, boneless and cubed
- 12 oz roasted red peppers, drained and chopped
- 1 tsp xanthan gum
- 1 tbsp tomato paste
- 5.4 oz coconut cream
- 10 garlic cloves
- 2/3 cup mayonnaise
- 5 zucchini, cut into cubes
- 1 tsp salt

Directions:

1. Add zucchini and chicken to a casserole dish. Cover dish with foil.
2. Select bake mode and set the omni to 400 F for 25 minutes once the oven beeps, place casserole dish into the oven.
3. Stir well and cook for 10 minutes more.
4. Meanwhile, in a bowl, stir together the remaining ingredients.
5. Pour bowl mixture over chicken and zucchini.
6. Serve and enjoy.

Nutritional Value (Amount per Serving):

- Calories 428
- Fat 21.9 g
- Carbohydrates 14.4 g
- Sugar 6.2 g
- Protein 43.9 g
- Cholesterol 131 mg

Chicken Fajita Casserole

Preparation Time: 5 minutes

Cooking Time: 30 minutes

Serve: 4

Ingredients:

- 1 lb cooked chicken, shredded
- 7 oz shredded cheese
- 2 tbsp tex-mex seasoning
- 1 onion, sliced
- 1 bell pepper, sliced
- 1/3 cup mayonnaise
- 7 oz cream cheese
- Pepper
- Salt

Directions:

1. Spray a baking dish with butter and set aside.
2. Mix all ingredients except 2 oz shredded cheese in a prepared baking dish.
3. Spread remaining cheese on top.
4. Select bake mode and set the omni to 400 F for 15 minutes once the oven beeps, place the baking dish into the oven.
5. Serve and enjoy.

Nutritional Value (Amount per Serving):

- Calories 641
- Fat 43.8 g
- Carbohydrates 11.5 g
- Sugar 4.3 g
- Protein 49.7 g
- Cholesterol 199 mg

Tasty Chicken Tandoori

Preparation Time: 5 minutes

Cooking Time: 15 minutes

Serve: 4

Ingredients:

- 1 lb chicken tenders, cut in half
- 1 tsp paprika
- 1 tbsp garlic, minced
- 1 tbsp ginger, minced
- 1/4 cup yogurt
- 1 tsp garam masala
- 1 tsp turmeric
- 1 tsp cayenne pepper
- 1/4 cup parsley, chopped
- 1 tsp salt

Directions:

1. Add all ingredients into the large bowl and mix well. Place in refrigerator for 30 minutes.
2. Spray air fryer basket with cooking spray.
3. Add marinated chicken into the preheated air fryer basket.
4. Place air fryer basket into the oven and select air fry mode set omni to the 350 F for 15 minutes. Turn chicken after 10 minutes.
5. Serve and enjoy.

Nutritional Value (Amount per Serving):

- Calories 240
- Fat 8.9 g
- Carbohydrates 3.9 g
- Sugar 1.3 g
- Protein 34.2 g
- Cholesterol 102 mg

Juicy Spicy Chicken Wings

Preparation Time: 5 minutes

Cooking Time: 25 minutes

Serve: 4

Ingredients:

- 2 lbs chicken wings
- 1/2 tsp Worcestershire sauce
- 1/2 tsp Tabasco
- 6 tbsp butter, melted
- 12 oz hot sauce

Directions:

1. Spray air fryer basket with cooking spray.
2. Add chicken wings into the air fryer basket.
3. Place air fryer basket into the oven and select air fry mode set omni to the 380 F for 25 minutes. Stir twice.
4. Meanwhile, in a bowl, mix together hot sauce, Worcestershire sauce, and butter. Set aside.
5. Add cooked chicken wings into the sauce bowl and toss well.
6. Serve and enjoy.

Nutritional Value (Amount per Serving):

- Calories 594
- Fat 34.4 g
- Carbohydrates 1.6 g
- Sugar 1.2 g
- Protein 66.2 g
- Cholesterol 248 mg

Chapter 5: Vegetarian Recipes

Cheesy Broccoli Casserole

Preparation Time: 5 minutes

Cooking Time: 30 minutes

Serve: 6

Ingredients:

- 16 oz frozen broccoli florets, defrosted and drained
- 1/2 tsp onion powder
- 10.5 oz can cream of mushroom soup
- 1 cup cheddar cheese, shredded
- 1/3 cup unsweetened almond milk

For topping:

- 1 tbsp butter, melted
- 1/2 cup cracker crumbs

Directions:

1. Add all ingredients except topping ingredients into the casserole dish.
2. In a small bowl, mix together cracker crumbs and melted butter and sprinkle over the casserole dish mixture.
3. Select bake mode and set the omni to 350 F for 30 minutes once the oven beeps, place casserole dish into the oven.
4. Serve and enjoy.

Nutritional Value (Amount per Serving):

- Calories 193
- Fat 12.9 g
- Carbohydrates 10.5 g
- Sugar 2.4 g
- Protein 6.9 g
- Cholesterol 27 mg

Curried Cauliflower

Preparation Time: 10 minutes

Cooking Time: 15 minutes

Serve: 4

Ingredients:

- 2 lbs cauliflower, cut into florets
- 1 1/2 tsp curry powder
- 1 tbsp olive oil
- 1 tbsp cilantro, chopped
- 2 tsp fresh lemon juice
- 1 tsp kosher salt

Directions:

1. Toss cauliflower florets in a large bowl with olive oil.
2. Sprinkle cauliflower florets with curry powder and salt.
3. Spread cauliflower florets onto a cooking pan.
4. Select bake mode and set the omni to 425 F for 15 minutes once the oven beeps, place the cooking pan into the oven.
5. Return roasted cauliflower florets into the bowl and toss with cilantro and lemon juice.
6. Serve and enjoy.

Nutritional Value (Amount per Serving):

- Calories 90
- Fat 3.9 g
- Carbohydrates 12.5 g
- Sugar 5.5 g
- Protein 4.6 g
- Cholesterol 0 mg

Baby Potatoes

Preparation Time: 10 minutes

Cooking Time: 20 minutes

Serve: 2

Ingredients:

- 12 oz baby potatoes
- 1/4 tsp cumin
- 1/4 tsp paprika
- 1/4 tsp chili powder
- 1/2 tbsp olive oil
- 1/4 tsp garlic salt
- 1/4 tsp pepper
- 1/2 tsp kosher salt

Directions:

1. Add all ingredients into a zip-lock bag and shake well.
2. Transfer potatoes into the air fryer basket.
3. Place air fryer basket into the oven and select air fry mode set omni to the 370 F for 20 minutes. Stir twice.
4. Serve and enjoy.

Nutritional Value (Amount per Serving):

- Calories 133
- Fat 3.8 g
- Carbohydrates 22 g
- Sugar 0.2 g
- Protein 4.6 g
- Cholesterol 0 mg

Mac & Cheese

Preparation Time: 5 minutes

Cooking Time: 20 minutes

Serve: 10

Ingredients:

- 1 lb cooked macaroni
- 1/2 cup flour
- 1/2 cup butter
- 1/2 cup breadcrumbs
- 12 oz cheddar cheese, shredded
- 4 1/2 cups unsweetened almond milk
- Pepper
- Salt

Directions:

1. Melt butter in a pan over medium heat.
2. Remove pan from heat and slowly add flour, salt, and pepper in melted butter.
3. Add ½ cup milk and stir until well blended.
4. Return to heat and slowly add remaining milk.
5. Add cheese and stir until cheese is melted.
6. Pour over cooked macaroni and stir well.
7. Transfer macaroni in a casserole dish and sprinkle with breadcrumbs.
8. Place casserole dish in Instant Omni Air Fryer Oven Combo Bakes at 350 F for 15-20 minutes.
9. Serve and enjoy.

Nutritional Value (Amount per Serving):

- Calories 449
- Fat 23.1 g
- Carbohydrates 43.9 g
- Sugar 1.8 g
- Protein 16.3 g
- Cholesterol 60 mg

Baked Vegetables

Preparation Time: 5 minutes

Cooking Time: 20 minutes

Serve: 4

Ingredients:

- 4 bell peppers
- 2 cups mushrooms
- 1/4 tsp black pepper
- 2 tbsp olive oil
- 2 eggplants
- 1 tsp salt

Directions:

1. Cut all vegetables into the small bite-sized pieces and place in a baking dish.
2. Drizzle vegetables with olive oil and season with pepper and salt.
3. Select bake mode and set the omni to 390 F for 20 minutes once the oven beeps, place the baking dish into the oven.
4. Serve and enjoy.

Nutritional Value (Amount per Serving):

- Calories 174
- Fat 7.9 g
- Carbohydrates 26.3 g
- Sugar 14.8 g
- Protein 5 g
- Cholesterol 0 mg

Potato Casserole

Preparation Time: 5 minutes

Cooking Time: 35 minutes

Serve: 6

Ingredients:

- 5 eggs
- 1/2 cup cheddar cheese, shredded
- 2 medium potatoes, diced into 1/2-inch cubes
- 1 green bell pepper, diced
- 1 onion, chopped
- 1 tbsp olive oil
- 3/4 tsp pepper
- 3/4 tsp salt

Directions:

1. Spray 9*9-inch casserole dish with cooking spray and set aside.
2. Heat olive oil in a large pan over medium heat.
3. Add onion and sauté for 1 minute. Add potatoes, bell peppers, ½ tsp black pepper, and 1.2 tsp salt and sauté for 4 minutes more or until onions are softened.
4. Transfer sautéed vegetables to the prepared casserole dish and spread evenly.
5. In a bowl, whisk eggs, and remaining pepper and salt.
6. Pour egg mixture into the casserole dish and sprinkle cheddar cheese on top.
7. Select bake mode and set the omni to 350 F for 35 minutes once the oven beeps, place casserole dish into the oven.
8. Serve and enjoy.

Nutritional Value (Amount per Serving):

- Calories 174
- Fat 9.2 g
- Carbohydrates 14.9 g
- Sugar 2.9 g
- Protein 8.6 g
- Cholesterol 146 mg

Spinach Bake

Preparation Time: 10 minutes

Cooking Time: 10 minutes

Serve: 6

Ingredients:

- 10 oz baby spinach
- 1 cup cheddar cheese, shredded
- 1/2 cup mayonnaise
- 2/3 cup yogurt
- 1/4 cup parmesan cheese, shredded
- 1/2 onion, chopped
- 2 tsp garlic powder

Directions:

1. Spray a baking dish with cooking spray and set aside.
2. Add all ingredients into the mixing bowl and stir to combine and pour into the baking dish.
3. Select bake mode and set the omni to 400 F for 10 minutes once the oven beeps, place the baking dish into the oven.
4. Serve and enjoy.

Nutritional Value (Amount per Serving):

- Calories 203
- Fat 14.2 g
- Carbohydrates 10.3 g
- Sugar 4.1 g
- Protein 9.4 g
- Cholesterol 29 mg

Arugula Artichoke Dip

Preparation Time: 5 minutes

Cooking Time: 30 minutes

Serve: 4

Ingredients:

- 15 oz artichoke hearts, drained
- 1 tsp Worcestershire sauce
- 3 cups arugula, chopped
- 1 cup cheddar cheese, shredded
- 1 tbsp onion, minced
- 1/2 cup mayonnaise

Directions:

1. Add all ingredients into the blender and blend until smooth.
2. Pour artichoke mixture into baking dish.
3. Select bake mode and set the omni to 350 F for 30 minutes once the oven beeps, place the baking dish into the oven.
4. Serve with crackers and enjoy.

Nutritional Value (Amount per Serving):

- Calories 284
- Fat 19.4 g
- Carbohydrates 19.6 g
- Sugar 3.8 g
- Protein 11.2 g
- Cholesterol 37 mg

Zucchini Patties

Preparation Time: 5 minutes

Cooking Time: 15 minutes

Serve: 6

Ingredients:

- 1 egg, beaten
- 1/4 tsp garlic powder
- 1/4 tsp basil, dried
- 1 1/2 cups zucchini, shredded
- 1/4 cup breadcrumbs
- 1/4 cup cheddar cheese, shredded
- 1/8 tsp pepper
- 1/4 tsp salt

Directions:

1. Spray a cooking pan with cooking spray and set aside.
2. Place shredded zucchini on a paper towel and pat dry.
3. Add zucchini and remaining ingredients into the bowl and mix well.
4. Drop a tablespoon of mixture on a prepared cooking pan and lightly flatten with a spoon.
5. Select bake mode and set the omni to 425 F for 15 minutes once the oven beeps, place the cooking pan into the oven.
6. Serve and enjoy.

Nutritional Value (Amount per Serving):

- Calories 52
- Fat 2.6 g
- Carbohydrates 4.4 g
- Sugar 0.9 g
- Protein 3.1 g
- Cholesterol 32 mg

Delicious Potato Patties

Preparation Time: 10 minutes

Cooking Time: 8 minutes

Serve: 2

Ingredients:

- 1 egg, beaten
- 1/4 tsp onion powder
- 1/4 tsp garlic powder
- 1 cup mashed potatoes
- 2 tbsp green onion, chopped
- 1 cup breadcrumbs
- 1/2 cup flour
- 1/2 cup cheddar cheese, shredded
- Pepper
- Salt

Directions:

1. Spray cooking pan with cooking spray and set aside.
2. In a bowl, mix together mashed potatoes, green onion, cheese, onion powder, and garlic powder.
3. Add flour, egg, and breadcrumbs in three separate bowls.
4. Make patties from potato mixture then roll in flour, dip in eggs, and coat with breadcrumbs.
5. Place patties on a cooking pan.
6. Place cooking pan into the oven and select air fry mode set omni to the 370 F for 8 minutes.
7. Serve and enjoy.

Nutritional Value (Amount per Serving):

- Calories 577
- Fat 16.2 g
- Carbohydrates 83.8 g
- Sugar 4.1 g
- Protein 23.3 g
- Cholesterol 114 mg

Parmesan Hassel back Potatoes

Preparation Time: 10 minutes

Cooking Time: 40 minutes

Serve: 2

Ingredients:

- 2 potatoes, make the thin slices
- 2 tbsp butter, melted
- 3 tbsp mushrooms, sliced
- 4 tbsp parmesan cheese, grated
- Pepper
- Salt

Directions:

1. Spray the cooking pan with cooking spray and set aside.
2. Slide mushroom slices into each slit.
3. Place potatoes on cooking pan and brush with half-melted butter.
4. Place cooking pan into the oven and select air fry mode set omni to the 350 F for 20 minutes.
5. Turn potatoes to the other side and brush with remaining butter and air fry for 20 minutes more.
6. Sprinkle with parmesan cheese and serve.

Nutritional Value (Amount per Serving):

- Calories 345
- Fat 18 g
- Carbohydrates 34.8 g
- Sugar 2.6 g
- Protein 13.4 g
- Cholesterol 51 mg

Baked Egg Tomato

Preparation Time: 5 minutes

Cooking Time: 30 minutes

Serve: 2

Ingredients:

- 2 eggs
- 1 tsp fresh parsley
- 2 large fresh tomatoes
- Pepper
- Salt

Directions:

1. Cut the top of the tomato and spoon out the tomato innards.
2. Break the egg in each tomato. Place tomatoes on the cooking pan.
3. Select bake mode and set the omni to 350 F for 30 minutes once the oven beeps, place the cooking pan into the oven.
4. Season with pepper, and salt.
5. Garnish with parsley and serve.

Nutritional Value (Amount per Serving):

- Calories 96
- Fat 4.7 g
- Carbohydrates 7.5 g
- Sugar 5.1 g
- Protein 7.2 g
- Cholesterol 164 mg

Veggie Tots

Preparation Time: 10 minutes

Cooking Time: 10 minutes

Serve: 2

Ingredients:

- 1 egg
- 1 carrot, grated & squeeze out the liquid
- 1/4 cup breadcrumbs
- 1 zucchini, grated & squeeze out the liquid
- 1/4 cup parmesan cheese, grated
- Pepper
- Salt

Directions:

1. Spray air fryer basket with cooking spray.
2. Add all ingredients into the bowl and mix until well combined.
3. Make tots from mixture and place into the air fryer basket.
4. Place air fryer basket into the oven and select air fry mode set omni to the 400 F for 15 minutes.
5. Serve and enjoy.

Nutritional Value (Amount per Serving):

- Calories 153
- Fat 5.8 g
- Carbohydrates 16.7 g
- Sugar 4.2 g
- Protein 10 g
- Cholesterol 91 mg

Chapter 6: Meat Recipes

Beef Chickpea Stew

Preparation Time: 10 minutes

Cooking Time: 4 hours 10 minutes

Serve: 4

Ingredients:

- 16 oz can chickpeas, drained
- 1 onion, chopped
- 1/2 tsp dried rosemary, crushed
- 2 lbs stew beef, cut into cubes
- 1/2 cup chicken stock
- 10 oz can tomatoes, diced
- 1 carrot, peeled and sliced
- 1 tbsp olive oil
- Pepper
- Salt

Directions:

1. Heat oil in a pan over medium-high heat.
2. Add meat to the pan and cook until brown from all the sides. Season with rosemary, pepper, and salt.
3. Add onion to the pan and sauté until lightly brown.
4. Transfer meat mixture to the Dutch oven along with remaining ingredients and stir well.
5. Cover and place in Instant Omni Air Fryer Oven Combo.
6. Select slow cook mode and set the omni to low for 4 hours. Press start.
7. Serve and enjoy.

Nutritional Value (Amount per Serving):

- Calories 530
- Fat 18.5 g
- Carbohydrates 33.5 g
- Sugar 4.4 g
- Protein 56.7 g
- Cholesterol 0 mg

Meatballs

Preparation Time: 10 minutes

Cooking Time: 8 minutes

Serve: 10

Ingredients:

- 5.3 oz minced beef
- 2 oz feta cheese, crumbled
- 2 tbsp almond flour
- 1/2 tbsp lemon zest, grated
- 1 tbsp fresh oregano, chopped
- Pepper
- Salt

Directions:

1. Add all ingredients into the mixing bowl and mix until well combined.
2. Make small balls from the meat mixture.
3. Place meatballs into the air fryer basket.
4. Place air fryer basket into the oven and select air fry mode set omni to the 390 F for 8 minutes.
5. Serve and enjoy.

Nutritional Value (Amount per Serving):

- Calories 76
- Fat 5 g
- Carbohydrates 1.8 g
- Sugar 0.5 g
- Protein 6.6 g
- Cholesterol 18 mg

Delicious Beef with Artichokes

Preparation Time: 10 minutes

Cooking Time: 7 hours 10 minutes

Serve: 6

Ingredients:

- 2 lbs stew beef, cut into 1-inch cubes
- 1 bay leaf
- 14.5 oz can tomatoes, diced
- 15 oz can tomato sauce
- 32 oz chicken stock
- 3 garlic cloves, chopped
- 1 onion, diced
- 14 oz can artichoke hearts, drained and halved
- 1 tbsp olive oil
- 1/2 tsp ground cumin
- 1 tsp dried basil
- 1 tsp dried parsley
- 1 tsp dried oregano
- 1/2 cup olives, pitted and chopped

Directions:

1. Heat olive oil in a large pot over medium-high heat.
2. Add meat to the pot and cook until brown, about 2 minutes on each side.
3. Transfer meat to the Dutch oven. Pour remaining ingredients over the meat and stir well.
4. Cover and place in Instant Omni Air Fryer Oven Combo.
5. Select slow cook mode and set the omni to low for 7 hours. Press start.
6. Serve and enjoy.

Nutritional Value (Amount per Serving):

- Calories 322
- Fat 13.2 g
- Carbohydrates 14.3 g
- Sugar 7.1 g
- Protein 36.8 g
- Cholesterol 0 mg

Herb Butter Pork Chops

Preparation Time: 10 minutes

Cooking Time: 1 hour 15 minutes

Serve: 4

Ingredients:

- 4 pork chops, boneless
- 1/2 cup chicken broth
- 1/2 tsp dried parsley
- 1 1/2 tsp chives
- 1 tbsp butter
- 1 tbsp olive oil
- 1/2 tsp dried sage
- 1/4 tsp pepper
- 1/4 tsp salt

Directions:

1. Spray a baking dish with cooking spray and set aside.
2. Season pork chops with pepper and salt and place in prepared baking dish.
3. In a small bowl, mix together butter, oil, sage, parsley, and chives.
4. Rub butter mixture on top of each pork chops.
5. Add broth in the baking dish around the pork chops.
6. Cover baking dish with foil.
7. Select bake mode and set the omni to 350 F for 1 hour 15 minutes once the oven beeps, place the baking dish into the oven.
8. Serve and enjoy.

Nutritional Value (Amount per Serving):

- Calories 317
- Fat 26.4 g
- Carbohydrates 0.3 g
- Sugar 0.1 g
- Protein 18.7 g
- Cholesterol 76 mg

Cajun Pork Chops

Preparation Time: 10 minutes

Cooking Time: 10 minutes

Serve: 2

Ingredients:

- 2 pork chops, boneless
- 1 tsp paprika
- 3 tbsp parmesan cheese, grated
- 1/3 cup almond flour
- 1/2 tsp Cajun seasoning
- 1 tsp herb de Provence

Directions:

1. Mix together almond flour, Cajun seasoning, herb de Provence, paprika, and parmesan cheese.
2. Spray both the pork chops with cooking spray.
3. Coat both the pork chops with almond flour mixture and place on cooking pan.
4. Place cooking pan into the oven and select air fry mode set omni to the 350 F for 10 minutes.
5. Serve and enjoy.

Nutritional Value (Amount per Serving):

- Calories 355
- Fat 27 g
- Carbohydrates 2.4 g
- Sugar 0.3 g
- Protein 26.1 g
- Cholesterol 84 mg

Meatballs

Preparation Time: 10 minutes

Cooking Time: 15 minutes

Serve: 6

Ingredients:

- 2 eggs
- 30 oz ground beef
- 3 cheese sticks
- 1 tbsp Italian seasoning
- 1/4 cup parmesan cheese, grated
- Pepper
- Salt

Directions:

1. Spray air fryer basket with cooking spray.
2. In a bowl, mix together meat, seasoning, parmesan cheese, and egg. Cut cheese sticks into the pieces.
3. Take a handful of meat mixture and place one piece of cheese string inside and give a round ball shape.
4. Place meatballs into the air fryer basket.
5. Place air fryer basket into the oven and select air fry mode set omni to the 375 F for 15 minutes.
6. Serve and enjoy.

Nutritional Value (Amount per Serving):

- Calories 361
- Fat 16.5 g
- Carbohydrates 0.7 g
- Sugar 0.4 g
- Protein 49.7 g
- Cholesterol 201 mg

Tender Pork Tenderloin

Preparation Time: 10 minutes

Cooking Time: 35 minutes

Serve: 3

Ingredients:

- 1 lb pork tenderloin
- 1 tbsp olive oil
- 1/2 tbsp dried rosemary
- Pepper
- Salt

Directions:

1. Mix together rosemary and olive oil and rub over pork tenderloin.
2. Place pork tenderloin in baking dish.
3. Select bake mode and set the omni to 400 F for 35 minutes once the oven beeps, place the baking dish into the oven.
4. Remove from oven and season with pepper and salt.
5. Slice and serve.

Nutritional Value (Amount per Serving):

- Calories 258
- Fat 10.1 g
- Carbohydrates 0.4 g
- Sugar 0 g
- Protein 39.6 g
- Cholesterol 110 mg

Garlic Rosemary Pork Chops

Preparation Time: 10 minutes

Cooking Time: 30 minutes

Serve: 4

Ingredients:

- 4 pork chops, boneless
- 1 tsp dried rosemary, crushed
- 1 tbsp fresh rosemary, chopped
- 3 garlic cloves, minced
- 1/4 tsp pepper
- 1/4 tsp salt

Directions:

1. Spray a cooking pan with cooking spray and set aside.
2. Season pork chops with pepper and salt and set aside.
3. In a small bowl, mix together garlic and rosemary and rub over pork chops.
4. Place pork chops on cooking pan.
5. Select bake mode and set the omni to 350 F for 30 minutes once the oven beeps, place the cooking pan into the oven.
6. Serve and enjoy.

Nutritional Value (Amount per Serving):

- Calories 263
- Fat 20.1 g
- Carbohydrates 1.5 g
- Sugar 0 g
- Protein 18.2 g
- Cholesterol 69 mg

Garlic Pork Sirloin Roast

Preparation Time: 10 minutes

Cooking Time: 1 hour 15 minutes

Serve: 4

Ingredients:

- 2 lbs pork sirloin roast
- 2 tbsp olive oil
- 4 garlic cloves, sliced
- 1/2 tsp pepper
- 1 tsp salt

Directions:

1. Using a sharp knife make slits on top of roast and stuff sliced garlic in each slit. Season pork roast with pepper and salt.
2. Heat olive oil in a pan over medium-high heat.
3. Place roast on the hot pan and cook until brown from all the sides.
4. Transfer pork roast on a cooking pan.
5. Select bake mode and set the omni to 350 F for 60-70 minutes once the oven beeps, place cooking pan into the oven. Turn roast halfway through.
6. Slice and serve.

Nutritional Value (Amount per Serving):

- Calories 535
- Fat 28.4 g
- Carbohydrates 1.2 g
- Sugar 0 g
- Protein 64.9 g
- Cholesterol 195 mg

Paprika Pork Tenderloin

Preparation Time: 10 minutes

Cooking Time: 30 minutes

Serve: 6

Ingredients:

- 2 lbs pork tenderloin

For rub:

- 1 tbsp smoked paprika
- 1 tbsp garlic powder
- 1 tbsp onion powder
- 1/2 tsp salt

Directions:

1. In a small bowl, combine together all rub ingredients.
2. Coat pork tenderloin with the rub.
3. Heat ovenproof pan over medium-high heat. Spray pan with cooking spray. Sear pork on all sides until lightly golden brown.
4. Select bake mode and set the omni to 425 F for 30 minutes once the oven beeps, place the pan into the oven.
5. Slice and serve.

Nutritional Value (Amount per Serving):

- Calories 228
- Fat 5.5 g
- Carbohydrates 2.6 g
- Sugar 0.9 g
- Protein 40.1 g
- Cholesterol 110 mg

Oregano Lamb Chops

Preparation Time: 10 minutes

Cooking Time: 5 minutes

Serve: 2

Ingredients:

- 4 lamb chops
- 1 garlic clove, minced
- 1/2 tbsp fresh oregano, chopped
- 1 1/2 tbsp olive oil
- Pepper
- Salt

Directions:

1. Mix together garlic, olive oil, oregano, pepper, and salt and rub over lamb chops.
2. Place lamb chops on the cooking pan.
3. Place cooking pan into the oven and select air fry mode set omni to the 400 F for 5 minutes.
4. Serve and enjoy.

Nutritional Value (Amount per Serving):

- Calories 518
- Fat 27.3 g
- Carbohydrates 1.3 g
- Sugar 0.1 g
- Protein 63.9 g
- Cholesterol 204 mg

Easy Jerk Pork Butt

Preparation Time: 10 minutes

Cooking Time: 20 minutes

Serve: 4

Ingredients:

- 1 1/2 lbs pork butt, chopped into pieces
- 1/4 cup jerk paste

Directions:

1. Add meat and jerk paste into the bowl and mix well. Place in refrigerator overnight.
2. Spray cooking pan with cooking spray.
3. Place marinated meat on the cooking pan.
4. Place cooking pan into the oven and select air fry mode set omni to the 390 F for 20 minutes.
5. Serve and enjoy.

Nutritional Value (Amount per Serving):

- Calories 339
- Fat 12.1 g
- Carbohydrates 0.8 g
- Sugar 0.6 g
- Protein 53 g
- Cholesterol 156 mg

Burger Patties

Preparation Time: 10 minutes

Cooking Time: 45 minutes

Serve: 4

Ingredients:

- 10.5 oz beef mince
- 1 tsp basil
- 1 tsp mustard
- 1 tsp tomato puree
- 1 tsp garlic puree
- 1 oz cheddar cheese
- 1 tsp mixed herbs
- Pepper
- Salt

Directions:

1. Line cooking pan with parchment paper and set aside.
2. Add meat and remaining ingredients into the large bowl and mix until well combined.
3. Make four medium-size patties from meat mixture and place onto the cooking pan.
4. Place cooking pan into the oven and select air fry mode set omni to the 390 F for 25 minutes.
5. Turn patties to the other side and cook at 350 F for 20 minutes more.
6. Serve and enjoy.

Nutritional Value (Amount per Serving):

- Calories 173
- Fat 7.2 g
- Carbohydrates 0.8 g
- Sugar 0.2 g
- Protein 24.7 g
- Cholesterol 74 mg

Chapter 7: Seafood Recipes

Baked Tilapia

Preparation Time: 5 minutes

Cooking Time: 15 minutes

Serve: 4

Ingredients:

- 1 lb tilapia fillets
- 2 tbsp olive oil
- 2 tbsp dried parsley
- 2 tbsp garlic, minced
- Pepper
- Salt

Directions:

1. Spray cooking pan with cooking spray and set aside.
2. Place fish fillets on cooking pan. Drizzle with oil and season with pepper and salt.
3. Sprinkle garlic and parsley over fish fillets.
4. Select bake mode and set the omni to 400 F for 15 minutes once the oven beeps, place the cooking pan into the oven.
5. Serve and enjoy.

Nutritional Value (Amount per Serving):

- Calories 160
- Fat 8.1 g
- Carbohydrates 1.5 g
- Sugar 0.1 g
- Protein 21.4 g
- Cholesterol 55 mg

Lemon Garlic Tilapia

Preparation Time: 5 minutes

Cooking Time: 12 minutes

Serve: 4

Ingredients:

- 4 tilapia fillets
- 2 tbsp fresh parsley, chopped
- 1 lemon zest
- 2 tbsp fresh lemon juice
- 3 garlic cloves, minced
- 1/4 cup olive oil
- Pepper
- Salt

Directions:

1. Spray a baking dish with cooking spray and set aside.
2. In a small bowl, whisk together olive oil, lemon zest, lemon juice, and garlic.
3. Season fish fillets with pepper and salt and place onto the baking dish.
4. Pour olive oil mixture over fish fillets.
5. Select bake mode and set the omni to 425 F for 12 minutes once the oven beeps, place the baking dish into the oven.
6. Garnish with parsley and serve.

Nutritional Value (Amount per Serving):

- Calories 211
- Fat 13.8 g
- Carbohydrates 2.4 g
- Sugar 0.6 g
- Protein 21.4 g
- Cholesterol 55 mg

Sweet & Spicy Fish Fillets

Preparation Time: 5 minutes

Cooking Time: 15 minutes

Serve: 6

Ingredients:

- 1 1/2 lbs salmon fillets
- 3 tbsp brown sugar
- 2 tbsp fresh lime juice
- 1/3 cup olive oil
- 1/2 tsp red pepper flakes
- 2 garlic cloves, minced
- Pepper
- Salt

Directions:

1. Line cooking pan with parchment paper and set aside.
2. Place salmon on a prepared cooking pan and season with pepper and salt.
3. In a small bowl, whisk together oil, red pepper flakes, garlic, brown sugar, and lime juice.
4. Pour oil mixture over salmon.
5. Select bake mode and set the omni to 350 F for 15 minutes once the oven beeps, place the cooking pan into the oven.
6. Serve and enjoy.

Nutritional Value (Amount per Serving):

- Calories 269
- Fat 18.3 g
- Carbohydrates 6.1 g
- Sugar 4.7 g
- Protein 22.2 g
- Cholesterol 50 mg

Dijon Maple Salmon

Preparation Time: 5 minutes

Cooking Time: 10 minutes

Serve: 6

Ingredients:

- 1 lb salmon
- 3 tbsp maple syrup
- 3 tbsp olive oil
- 1 tsp ginger, grated
- 2 1/2 tbsp Dijon mustard
- 1 tsp pepper

Directions:

1. In a small bowl, mix together olive oil, mustard, maple syrup, ginger, and pepper.
2. Spray a baking dish with cooking spray and set aside.
3. Place salmon in a baking dish and spread olive oil mixture over salmon evenly.
4. Select bake mode and set the omni to 400 F for 10 minutes once the oven beeps, place the baking dish into the oven.
5. Serve and enjoy.

Nutritional Value (Amount per Serving):

- Calories 192
- Fat 12 g
- Carbohydrates 7.5 g
- Sugar 6 g
- Protein 15 g
- Cholesterol 33 mg

Baked Lemon Cod

Preparation Time: 5 minutes

Cooking Time: 10 minutes

Serve: 2

Ingredients:

- 1 lb cod fillets, rinsed and pat dry
- 1/8 tsp cayenne pepper
- 1 tbsp fresh lemon juice
- 1 tbsp fresh parsley, chopped
- 1 1/2 tbsp olive oil
- 1/4 tsp salt

Directions:

1. Arrange fish fillets on cooking pan. Drizzle with oil and lemon juice and season with cayenne pepper and salt.
2. Select bake mode and set the omni to 400 F for 10 minutes once the oven beeps, place the cooking pan into the oven.
3. Garnish with parsley and serve.

Nutritional Value (Amount per Serving):

- Calories 275
- Fat 11.6 g
- Carbohydrates 0.3 g
- Sugar 0.2 g
- Protein 44.7 g
- Cholesterol 71 mg

Air Fryer Salmon

Preparation Time: 5 minutes

Cooking Time: 7 minutes

Serve: 2

Ingredients:

- 2 salmon fillets, remove bones
- 2 tsp olive oil
- 2 tsp paprika
- Pepper
- Salt

Directions:

1. Rub each salmon fillet with oil, paprika, pepper, and salt.
2. Place salmon fillets in the air fryer basket
3. Place air fryer basket into the oven and select air fry mode set omni to the 390 F for 7 minutes.
4. Serve and enjoy.

Nutritional Value (Amount per Serving):

- Calories 282
- Fat 15.9 g
- Carbohydrates 1.2 g
- Sugar 0.2 g
- Protein 34.9 g
- Cholesterol 78 mg

Greek Fish

Preparation Time: 5 minutes

Cooking Time: 15 minutes

Serve: 4

Ingredients:

- 4 halibut fish fillets
- 2 tsp olive oil
- 3 tbsp fresh basil, chopped
- 2 tomatoes, chopped
- 2 garlic cloves, minced
- 1 tsp oregano, chopped

Directions:

1. Spray a baking dish with cooking spray and set aside.
2. In a bowl, mix together chopped tomatoes, garlic, oregano, and basil.
3. Arrange fish fillets in a baking dish and top with tomato mixture.
4. Select bake mode and set the omni to 350 F for 15 minutes once the oven beeps, place the baking dish into the oven.
5. Serve and enjoy.

Nutritional Value (Amount per Serving):

- Calories 445
- Fat 22.5 g
- Carbohydrates 35.2 g
- Sugar 1.7 g
- Protein 25.7 g
- Cholesterol 10 mg

Tomato Basil Fish

Preparation Time: 5 minutes

Cooking Time: 19 minutes

Serve: 2

Ingredients:

- 2 cod fillets
- 1 tsp olive oil
- 1 tbsp fresh lemon juice
- 2 tsp parmesan cheese, grated
- 2 tomatoes, sliced
- 1/4 tsp dried basil
- 1/8 tsp pepper
- 1/8 tsp salt

Directions:

1. Place fish fillets in greased baking dish.
2. Mix together oil and lemon juice and drizzle over fish fillets. Season fish with basil, pepper, and salt.
3. Arrange tomato slices on top of fish fillets.
4. Sprinkle grated parmesan cheese on top. Cover dish with foil.
5. Select bake mode and set the omni to 400 F for 12 minutes once the oven beeps, place the baking dish into the oven.
6. Serve and enjoy.

Nutritional Value (Amount per Serving):

- Calories 182
- Fat 6.3 g
- Carbohydrates 5.6 g
- Sugar 3.4 g
- Protein 27.9 g
- Cholesterol 46 mg

Pesto Salmon

Preparation Time: 5 minutes

Cooking Time: 20 minutes

Serve: 2

Ingredients:

- 2 salmon fillets
- 1/4 cup parmesan cheese, grated

For pesto:

- 1/4 cup parmesan cheese, grated
- 1/4 cup pine nuts
- 1/4 cup olive oil
- 1 1/2 cups fresh basil leaves
- 2 garlic cloves, peeled and chopped
- 1/2 tsp pepper
- 1/2 tsp salt

Directions:

1. Add all pesto ingredients into the food processor and process until smooth.
2. Place salmon fillets in a baking dish and spread 2 tablespoons of the pesto on each salmon fillet.
3. Sprinkle grated cheese on top of the pesto.
4. Select bake mode and set the omni to 400 F for 20 minutes once the oven beeps, place the baking dish into the oven.
5. Serve and enjoy.

Nutritional Value (Amount per Serving):

- Calories 616
- Fat 50.7 g
- Carbohydrates 4.5 g
- Sugar 0.7 g
- Protein 41.7 g
- Cholesterol 87 mg

Chili Garlic Shrimp

Preparation Time: 5 minutes

Cooking Time: 7

Serve: 4

Ingredients:

- 1 lb shrimp, peeled and deveined
- 1 tbsp olive oil
- 1 lemon, sliced
- 1 red chili, sliced
- 1/2 tsp garlic powder
- Pepper
- Salt

Directions:

1. Spray air fryer basket with cooking spray.
2. Add all ingredients into the mixing bowl and toss well.
3. Transfer shrimp mixture into the air fryer basket.
4. Place air fryer basket into the oven and select air fry mode set omni to the 400 F for 7 minutes. Stir halfway through.
5. Serve and enjoy.

Nutritional Value (Amount per Serving):

- Calories 171
- Fat 5.5 g
- Carbohydrates 3.4 g
- Sugar 0.5 g
- Protein 26.1 g
- Cholesterol 239 mg

Simple Salmon Patties

Preparation Time: 5 minutes

Cooking Time: 10 minutes

Serve: 2

Ingredients:

- 1 egg
- 14.5 oz salmon
- 1 tsp dill weed
- 1/2 cup almond flour
- 1/4 cup onion, diced

Directions:

1. Spray air fryer basket with cooking spray.
2. Add all ingredients into the mixing bowl and mix well.
3. Make patties from bowl mixture and place it into the air fryer basket.
4. Place air fryer basket into the oven and select air fry mode set omni to the 370 F for 10 minutes. Turn patties halfway through.
5. Serve and enjoy.

Nutritional Value (Amount per Serving):

- Calories 350
- Fat 18.4 g
- Carbohydrates 3.3 g
- Sugar 1 g
- Protein 44.4 g
- Cholesterol 172 mg

Chapter 8: Snacks & Appetizers

Spicy Almonds

Preparation Time: 10 minutes

Cooking Time: 20 minutes

Serve: 6

Ingredients:

- 1 1/2 cups raw almonds
- 1/2 tsp cayenne
- 1/4 tsp onion powder
- 1/4 tsp dried basil
- 1/2 tsp garlic powder
- 1/2 tsp cumin
- 1 1/2 tsp chili powder
- 2 tsp Worcestershire sauce
- 2 tbsp butter, melted
- 1/2 tsp sea salt

Directions:

1. Line cooking pan with parchment paper and set aside.
2. In a mixing bowl, whisk together butter, Worcestershire sauce, chili powder, cumin, garlic powder, basil, onion powder, cayenne, and salt.
3. Add almonds and toss to coat.
4. Spread almonds onto the prepared cooking pan.
5. Select bake mode and set the omni to 350 F for 20 minutes once the oven beeps, place the cooking pan into the oven.
6. Serve and enjoy.

Nutritional Value (Amount per Serving):

- Calories 117
- Fat 15.9 g
- Carbohydrates 6.2 g
- Sugar 1.5 g
- Protein 5.2 g
- Cholesterol 10 mg

Buffalo Chicken Dip

Preparation Time: 10 minutes

Cooking Time: 10 minutes

Serve: 8

Ingredients:

- 2 can chunk chicken, drained
- 2 cups cheddar cheese, shredded
- 1 cup ranch dressing
- 1 package cream cheese
- 3/4 cup hot sauce

Directions:

1. Add chicken and hot sauce to the pan and cook for 2 minutes.
2. Add cream and ranch dressing and stir well.
3. Add half cheese and stir until well blended.
4. Transfer chicken mixture to the baking dish and sprinkle the remaining cheese on top.
5. Select bake mode and set the omni to 370 F for 10 minutes once the oven beeps, place the baking dish into the oven.
6. Serve and enjoy.

Nutritional Value (Amount per Serving):

- Calories 514
- Fat 18 g
- Carbohydrates 4 g
- Sugar 2 g
- Protein 24 g
- Cholesterol 113 mg

Tasty Zucchini Fritters

Preparation Time: 10 minutes

Cooking Time: 25 minutes

Serve: 4

Ingredients:

- 1 egg
- 1 tsp garlic powder
- 2 tbsp dill, chopped
- 3 tbsp chives, chopped
- 1/4 cup parmesan cheese, grated
- 1/2 cup cheddar cheese, shredded
- 1 1/4 cups oat flour
- 2 medium zucchini, shredded and squeeze out all liquid
- 1 tsp kosher salt

Directions:

1. Line cooking pan with parchment paper and set aside.
2. Add all ingredients into the mixing bowl and mix until well combined.
3. Make small patties from mixture and place onto the prepared cooking pan.
4. Select bake mode and set the omni to 375 F for 25 minutes once the oven beeps, place the cooking pan into the oven.
5. Serve and enjoy.

Nutritional Value (Amount per Serving):

- Calories 228
- Fat 9.3 g
- Carbohydrates 24.9 g
- Sugar 2.1 g
- Protein 12.4 g
- Cholesterol 60 mg

Easy Roasted Walnuts

Preparation Time: 10 minutes

Cooking Time: 5 minutes

Serve: 6

Ingredients:

- 2 cups walnuts
- 1/4 tsp chili powder
- 1/8 tsp paprika
- 1 tsp olive oil
- Pepper
- Salt

Directions:

1. Add walnuts, chili powder, paprika, oil, pepper, and salt into the bowl and toss well.
2. Spread walnuts onto the cooking pan.
3. Place cooking pan into the oven and select air fry mode set omni to the 320 F for 5 minutes.
4. Serve and enjoy.

Nutritional Value (Amount per Serving):

- Calories 265
- Fat 25.4 g
- Carbohydrates 4.2 g
- Sugar 0.5 g
- Protein 10.1 g
- Cholesterol 0 mg

Artichoke Dip

Preparation Time: 10 minutes

Cooking Time: 30 minutes

Serve: 8

Ingredients:

- 2 cups mayonnaise
- 8 oz parmesan cheese, grated
- 7 oz can green chiles, diced
- 15 oz can artichoke hearts, drained and chopped

Directions:

1. Add all ingredients into the mixing bowl and mix until well combined.
2. Pour mixture into the 2-quart baking dish.
3. Select bake mode and set the omni to 325 F for 30 minutes once the oven beeps, place the baking dish into the oven.
4. Serve and enjoy.

Nutritional Value (Amount per Serving):

- Calories 340
- Fat 25.7 g
- Carbohydrates 18.5 g
- Sugar 5 g
- Protein 10.5 g
- Cholesterol 36 mg

Cheese Dip

Preparation Time: 10 minutes

Cooking Time: 10 minutes

Serve: 4

Ingredients:

- 10 oz goat cheese
- 2 tbsp olive oil
- 1/4 cup parmesan cheese
- 2 garlic cloves, minced
- 1/4 tsp sage
- 1/4 tsp thyme
- Pepper
- Salt

Directions:

1. Spray a baking dish with cooking spray and set aside.
2. Add all ingredients into the food processor and process until just combined.
3. Pour mixture into the prepared baking dish and spread well.
4. Select bake mode and set the omni to 400 F for 10 minutes once the oven beeps, place the baking dish into the oven.
5. Serve and enjoy.

Nutritional Value (Amount per Serving):

- Calories 403
- Fat 33.6 g
- Carbohydrates 2.3 g
- Sugar 1.6 g
- Protein 23.8 g
- Cholesterol 79 mg

Ranch Chickpeas

Preparation Time: 10 minutes

Cooking Time: 12 minutes

Serve: 12

Ingredients:

- 15 oz can chickpeas, rinsed, drained, and pat dry
- 2 tbsp ranch seasoning
- 1 tsp olive oil

Directions:

1. Line cooking pan with parchment paper and set aside.
2. In a mixing bowl, toss chickpeas with ranch seasoning and oil.
3. Spread chickpeas onto the prepared cooking pan.
4. Place cooking pan into the oven and select air fry mode set omni to the 380 F for 12 minutes. Stir chickpeas twice.
5. Serve and enjoy.

Nutritional Value (Amount per Serving):

- Calories 51
- Fat 0.8 g
- Carbohydrates 8 g
- Sugar 0 g
- Protein 1.8 g
- Cholesterol 0 mg

Parmesan Potatoes

Preparation Time: 10 minutes

Cooking Time: 45 minutes

Serve: 2

Ingredients:

- 5 medium potatoes, peeled and cut into 1/2-inch pieces
- 3 tbsp olive oil
- 1 tsp garlic powder
- 1 tsp paprika
- 1/2 cup parmesan cheese, grated
- Salt

Directions:

1. Line cooking pan with parchment paper and set aside.
2. In a mixing bowl, add potatoes and remaining ingredients and toss to coat.
3. Arrange potatoes on a prepared cooking pan.
4. Select bake mode and set the omni to 450 F for 30 minutes once the oven beeps, place the cooking pan into the oven.
5. Turn potatoes and bake for 10-15 minutes more.
6. Serve and enjoy.

Nutritional Value (Amount per Serving):

- Calories 635
- Fat 27 g
- Carbohydrates 86.2 g
- Sugar 6.6 g
- Protein 17.4 g
- Cholesterol 18 mg

Creamy Zucchini Dip

Preparation Time: 10 minutes

Cooking Time: 15 minutes

Serve: 6

Ingredients:

- 1 lb zucchini, grated & squeeze out all liquid
- 1 tbsp lime juice
- 1 tbsp olive oil
- 1 cup heavy cream
- 1 tsp garlic, minced
- 1 tsp dill, chopped
- Pepper
- Salt

Directions:

1. Spray a baking dish with cooking spray and set aside.
2. Add all ingredients into the large bowl and mix until well combined.
3. Pour zucchini mixture into the prepared baking dish.
4. Place baking dish into the oven and select air fry mode set omni to the 375 F for 15 minutes.
5. Serve and enjoy.

Nutritional Value (Amount per Serving):

- Calories 104
- Fat 9.9 g
- Carbohydrates 4 g
- Sugar 1.5 g
- Protein 1.4 g
- Cholesterol 27 mg

Cauliflower Hummus

Preparation Time: 10 minutes

Cooking Time: 35 minutes

Serve: 8

Ingredients:

- 1 cauliflower head, cut into florets
- 3 tbsp olive oil
- 1/2 tsp ground cumin
- 1 tsp garlic, chopped
- 2 tbsp fresh lemon juice
- 1/3 cup tahini
- Pepper
- Salt

Directions:

1. Spray cooking pan with cooking spray.
2. Spread cauliflower florets onto the prepared cooking pan.
3. Select bake mode and set the omni to 400 F for 35 minutes once the oven beeps, place the cooking pan into the oven. Turn cauliflower florets halfway through.
4. Transfer cauliflower florets into the food processor along with remaining ingredients and process until smooth.
5. Serve and enjoy.

Nutritional Value (Amount per Serving):

- Calories 115
- Fat 10.7 g
- Carbohydrates 4.2 g
- Sugar 0.9 g
- Protein 2.4 g
- Cholesterol 0 mg

Sweet & Spicy Mixed Nuts

Preparation Time: 10 minutes

Cooking Time: 20 minutes

Serve: 16

Ingredients:

- 4 cups mixed nuts
- 2 tbsp butter
- 1 tbsp maple syrup
- 1 tsp chili powder
- 1 1/2 tsp salt

Directions:

1. In a mixing bowl, mix together melted butter, maple syrup, chili powder, and salt.
2. Add mixed nuts and toss to coat.
3. Spread nuts onto the parchment-lined cooking pan
4. Select bake mode and set the omni to 300 F for 20 minutes once the oven beeps, place the cooking pan into the oven.
5. Serve and enjoy.

Nutritional Value (Amount per Serving):

- Calories 238
- Fat 21.7 g
- Carbohydrates 9 g
- Sugar 2.3 g
- Protein 5.6 g
- Cholesterol 4 mg

Easy Roasted Brussels Sprouts

Preparation Time: 10 minutes

Cooking Time: 35 minutes

Serve: 6

Ingredients:

- 2 cups Brussels sprouts, halved
- 1/4 tsp garlic powder
- 1/4 cup olive oil
- 1/4 tsp cayenne pepper
- 1/4 tsp salt

Directions:

1. Add all ingredients into the large bowl and toss well.
2. Transfer Brussels sprouts on a cooking pan.
3. Select bake mode and set the omni to 400 F for 35 minutes once the oven beeps, place the cooking pan into the oven. Turn halfway through.
4. Serve and enjoy.

Nutritional Value (Amount per Serving):

- Calories 85
- Fat 8.5 g
- Carbohydrates 2.8 g
- Sugar 0.7 g
- Protein 1 g
- Cholesterol 0 mg

Spicy Mix Nuts

Preparation Time: 10 minutes

Cooking Time: 4 minutes

Serve: 2

Ingredients:

- 2 cup mixed nuts
- 1 tsp ground cumin
- 1 tbsp olive oil
- 1 tsp chili powder
- 1 tsp pepper
- 1 tsp salt

Directions:

1. Add nuts and remaining ingredients into the mixing bowl and toss well.
2. Spread nuts onto the cooking pan.
3. Place cooking pan into the oven and select air fry mode set omni to the 350 F for 4 minutes. Stir halfway through.
4. Serve and enjoy.

Nutritional Value (Amount per Serving):

- Calories 956
- Fat 88.4 g
- Carbohydrates 33.9 g
- Sugar 8.8 g
- Protein 22.8 g
- Cholesterol 0 mg

Chapter 9: Dehydrated Recipes

Tasty Pineapple Chunks

Preparation Time: 10 minutes

Cooking Time: 12 hours

Serve: 4

Ingredients:

- 1 ripe pineapple, peel and cut in half

Directions:

1. Cut pineapple into the 1/4-inch to 1/2-inch thick chunks.
2. Arrange pineapple chunks on cooking pan in a single layer.
3. Place cooking pan in an Instant Omni Air Fryer Oven Combo. Select dehydrate mode and set the omni to 135 F for 12 hours.
4. Serve and enjoy.

Nutritional Value (Amount per Serving):

- Calories 21
- Fat 0.1 g
- Carbohydrates 5.4 g
- Sugar 4.1 g
- Protein 0.2 g
- Cholesterol 0 mg

Smoky Eggplant Bacon

Preparation Time: 10 minutes

Cooking Time: 4 hours

Serve: 4

Ingredients:

- 1 medium eggplant
- 1/4 tsp onion powder
- 1/4 tsp garlic powder
- 1 1/2 tsp smoked paprika

Directions:

1. Cut eggplant into the 1/4-inch thick slices.
2. Toss eggplant slices with onion powder, garlic powder, and paprika in a mixing bowl.
3. Arrange eggplant slices on cooking pan in a single layer.
4. Place cooking pan in an Instant Omni Air Fryer Oven Combo. Select dehydrate mode and set the omni to 145 F for 4 hours.
5. Serve and enjoy.

Nutritional Value (Amount per Serving):

- Calories 32
- Fat 0.3 g
- Carbohydrates 7.4 g
- Sugar 3.6 g
- Protein 1.3 g
- Cholesterol 0 mg

Cinnamon Sweet Potato Chips

Preparation Time: 10 minutes

Cooking Time: 12 hours

Serve: 2

Ingredients:

- 2 sweet potatoes, peel and sliced thinly
- 1 tsp coconut oil, melted
- 1/8 tsp ground cinnamon
- Salt

Directions:

1. Add sweet potato slices in a mixing bowl.
2. Add cinnamon, coconut oil, and salt and toss well.
3. Arrange sweet potato slices on cooking pan in a single layer.
4. Place cooking pan in an Instant Omni Air Fryer Oven Combo. Select dehydrate mode and set the omni to 125 F for 12 hours.

Nutritional Value (Amount per Serving):

- Calories 197
- Fat 2.5 g
- Carbohydrates 41.9 g
- Sugar 0.8 g
- Protein 2.3 g
- Cholesterol 0 mg

Dehydrated Banana Slices

Preparation Time: 10 minutes

Cooking Time: 8 hours

Serve: 4

Ingredients:

- 2 bananas, cut into 1/8-inch thick slices
- 1/2 cup fresh lemon juice

Directions:

1. Add sliced bananas and lemon juice in a mixing bowl and mix well.
2. Arrange sliced bananas on cooking pan in a single layer
3. Place cooking pan in an Instant Omni Air Fryer Oven Combo. Select dehydrate mode and set the omni to 135 F for 8 hours.

Nutritional Value (Amount per Serving):

- Calories 60
- Fat 0.4 g
- Carbohydrates 14.1 g
- Sugar 7.9 g
- Protein 0.9 g
- Cholesterol 0 mg

Spicy Kale Chips

Preparation Time: 10 minutes

Cooking Time: 11 hours

Serve: 4 cups

Ingredients:

- 5 oz fresh kale leaves

For sauce:

- 1 chipotle pepper
- 2 tbsp lemon juice
- 1 cup of water
- 1/2 cup sunflower seeds
- 1 cup cashews
- 1/4 tsp salt

Directions:

1. Add all sauce ingredients into the blender and blend until smooth.
2. Add kale leaves into the mixing bowl. Pour sauce over kale leaves mix until kale leaves are well coated with sauce.
3. Line cooking pan with parchment paper.
4. Arrange kale leaves on the cooking pan in a single layer.
5. Place cooking pan in an Instant Omni Air Fryer Oven Combo. Select dehydrate mode and set the omni to 155 F for 1 hour.
6. Turn temperature to 115 F and set a timer for 10 hours.
7. Serve and enjoy.

Nutritional Value (Amount per Serving):

- Calories 254
- Fat 18.9 g
- Carbohydrates 17.3 g
- Sugar 2.6 g
- Protein 7.8 g
- Cholesterol 0 mg

Easy Chicken Jerky

Preparation Time: 10 minutes

Cooking Time: 7 hours

Serve: 4

Ingredients:

- 1 lb chicken tenders, boneless, skinless and cut into 1/4-inch slices
- 1/2 tsp garlic powder
- 1 tsp lemon juice
- 1/2 cup soy sauce
- 1/4 tsp ground ginger
- 1/4 tsp black pepper

Directions:

1. Mix all ingredients except chicken slices into the zip-lock bag.
2. Add chicken and seal bag and mix well. Place the bag in the refrigerator for 30 minutes.
3. Arrange chicken slices on cooking pan in a single layer.
4. Place cooking pan in an Instant Omni Air Fryer Oven Combo. Select dehydrate mode and set the omni to 145 F for 7 hours.

Nutritional Value (Amount per Serving):

- Calories 235
- Fat 8.4 g
- Carbohydrates 2.9 g
- Sugar 0.7 g
- Protein 34.9 g
- Cholesterol 101 mg

Dehydrated Avocado Slices

Preparation Time: 10 minutes

Cooking Time: 10 hours

Serve: 4

Ingredients:

- 4 avocados, halved and pitted
- 1/4 tsp cayenne pepper
- 2 tbsp fresh cilantro, chopped
- 1/2 lemon juice
- 1/4 tsp sea salt

Directions:

1. Cut avocado into the slices. Drizzle lemon juice over avocado slices.
2. Arrange avocado slices on cooking pan in a single layer.
3. Place cooking pan in an Instant Omni Air Fryer Oven Combo. Select dehydrate mode and set the omni to 160 F for 10 hours.

Nutritional Value (Amount per Serving):

- Calories 412
- Fat 39.3 g
- Carbohydrates 17.5 g
- Sugar 1.1 g
- Protein 3.9 g
- Cholesterol 0 mg

Dehydrated Strawberry Slices

Preparation Time: 10 minutes

Cooking Time: 12 hours

Serve: 4

Ingredients:

- 2 cups strawberries, cut into 1/4-inch thick slices

Directions:

1. Arrange strawberry slices on cooking pan in a single layer.
2. Place cooking pan in an Instant Omni Air Fryer Oven Combo. Select dehydrate mode and set the omni to 135 F for 12 hours.

Nutritional Value (Amount per Serving):

- Calories 23
- Fat 0.2 g
- Carbohydrates 5.5 g
- Sugar 3.5 g
- Protein 0.5 g
- Cholesterol 0 mg

Squash Chips

Preparation Time: 5 minutes

Cooking Time: 12 hours

Serve: 8

Ingredients:

- 2 cups yellow squash, sliced 1/8-inch thick
- 2 tbsp apple cider vinegar
- 2 tsp olive oil
- Salt

Directions:

1. In a mixing bowl, mix squash slices, vinegar, oil, and salt.
2. Arrange squash slices on cooking pan in a single layer.
3. Place cooking pan in an Instant Omni Air Fryer Oven Combo. Select dehydrate mode and set the omni to 110 F for 12 hours.
4. Serve and enjoy.

Nutritional Value (Amount per Serving):

- Calories 15
- Fat 1.2 g
- Carbohydrates 1 g
- Sugar 0.5 g
- Protein 0.3 g
- Cholesterol 0 mg

Dehydrated Bell Peppers

Preparation Time: 10 minutes

Cooking Time: 24 hours

Serve: 4

Ingredients:

- 4 bell peppers, cut in half and remove seeds

Directions:

1. Cut bell peppers in strips then cut each strip in 1/2-inch pieces.
2. Arrange bell pepper strips on cooking pan in a single layer.
3. Place cooking pan in an Instant Omni Air Fryer Oven Combo. Select dehydrate mode and set the omni to 135 F for 24 hours.

Nutritional Value (Amount per Serving):

- Calories 38
- Fat 0.3 g
- Carbohydrates 9 g
- Sugar 6 g
- Protein 1.2 g
- Cholesterol 0 mg

Simple Kale Chips

Preparation Time: 10 minutes

Cooking Time: 4 hours

Serve: 4

Ingredients:

- 2 kale heads, wash and cut into bits
- 1 tbsp fresh lemon juice
- 3 tbsp nutritional yeast
- 2 tbsp olive oil
- 1 tsp garlic powder
- 1 tsp sea salt

Directions:

1. Add kale and remaining ingredients into the bowl and mix until well coated.
2. Arrange kale bits on cooking pan in a single layer.
3. Place cooking pan in an Instant Omni Air Fryer Oven Combo. Select dehydrate mode and set the omni to 145 F for 4 hours.

Nutritional Value (Amount per Serving):

- Calories 111
- Fat 7.5 g
- Carbohydrates 8.5 g
- Sugar 0.3 g
- Protein 4.9 g
- Cholesterol 0 mg

Dehydrated Shredded Carrots

Preparation Time: 10 minutes

Cooking Time: 10 hours

Serve: 4

Ingredients:

- 10 oz shredded carrots
- 2 tbsp coconut oil, melted
- 1/2 tsp ground cinnamon
- 1 tbsp sugar
- 1/2 tsp sea salt

Directions:

1. Add melted coconut oil in a large mixing bowl.
2. Add sugar, cinnamon, and salt to the bowl and stir well.
3. Add shredded carrots to the bowl and mix well to coat.
4. Arrange shredded carrots on cooking pan in a single layer
5. Place cooking pan in an Instant Omni Air Fryer Oven Combo. Select dehydrate mode and set the omni to 125 F for 10 hours.

Nutritional Value (Amount per Serving):

- Calories 100
- Fat 6.8 g
- Carbohydrates 10.2 g
- Sugar 6.5 g
- Protein 0.6 g
- Cholesterol 0 mg

Chapter 10: Desserts

Moist & Light Chocolate Cake

Preparation Time: 10 minutes

Cooking Time: 40 minutes

Serve: 18

Ingredients:

- 3 cups flour
- 2 cups cold water
- 2 tbsp white vinegar
- 2 tsp vanilla
- 10 tbsp oil
- 2 tsp baking soda
- 5 tbsp cocoa powder
- 2 cups of sugar
- 1 tsp salt

Directions:

1. Add all ingredients into the mixing bowl and mix until well combined.
2. Pour batter into the 9*13-inch cake pan.
3. Select bake mode and set the toaster oven to 350 F for 40 minutes once the oven beeps, place the cake pan into the oven.
4. Top with fresh whipped cream.
5. Slice and serve.

Nutritional Value (Amount per Serving):

- Calories 231
- Fat 8 g
- Carbohydrates 39 g
- Sugar 22.4 g
- Protein 2.4 g
- Cholesterol 0 mg

Delicious Peach Cobbler

Preparation Time: 10 minutes

Cooking Time: 60 minutes

Serve: 6

Ingredients:

- 3 cups peaches, peeled and sliced
- 1/4 tsp ground nutmeg
- 1/2 tsp ground cinnamon
- 1 cup milk
- 1 cup of sugar
- 1 1/4 cup Bisquick
- 1/2 cup butter, melted

Directions:

1. Grease 8-inch baking dish with cooking spray and set aside.
2. Arrange peaches in prepared baking dish. Stir together milk, butter, sugar, Bisquick, cinnamon, and nutmeg and pour over peach slices.
3. Select bake mode and set the omni to 350 F for 60 minutes once the oven beeps, place the baking dish into the oven.
4. Serve and enjoy.

Nutritional Value (Amount per Serving):

- Calories 413
- Fat 20.1 g
- Carbohydrates 57.6 g
- Sugar 45 g
- Protein 4.1 g
- Cholesterol 44 mg

Fudgy Cocoa Brownies

Preparation Time: 10 minutes

Cooking Time: 20 minutes

Serve: 16

Ingredients:

- 2 eggs
- 1/2 cup flour
- 1 tsp vanilla
- 1 cup of sugar
- 1/2 cup unsweetened cocoa powder
- 1/2 cup butter, melted
- 1/4 tsp salt

Directions:

1. Grease 8*8-inch pan and set aside.
2. In a mixing bowl, add butter, sugar, and cocoa powder and stir until sugar is dissolved.
3. Add eggs one by one. Add vanilla and stir until well combined.
4. Add flour and salt and stir until just combined.
5. Pour batter into the prepared pan.
6. Select bake mode and set the omni to 350 F for 20 minutes once the oven beeps, place the pan into the oven.
7. Slice and serve.

Nutritional Value (Amount per Serving):

- Calories 127
- Fat 6.7 g
- Carbohydrates 17 g
- Sugar 12.6 g
- Protein 1.7 g
- Cholesterol 36 mg

Blueberry Muffins

Preparation Time: 10 minutes

Cooking Time: 30 minutes

Serve: 12

Ingredients:

- 2 eggs
- 2 1/2 cups blueberries
- 2 tsp baking powder
- 3/4 cup sugar
- 2 cups all-purpose flour
- 1/2 cup milk
- 8 tbsp butter, melted
- 1 tsp kosher salt

Directions:

1. Line muffin tray with cupcake liners and set aside.
2. In a mixing bowl, whisk together eggs, butter, and milk.
3. In a large bowl, mix together flour, baking powder, sugar, and salt.
4. Add egg mixture into the flour mixture and mix until well combined.
5. Add blueberries and fold well. Pour batter into the prepared muffin tray.
6. Select bake mode and set the omni to 375 F for 30 minutes once the oven beeps, place muffin tray into the oven.
7. Serve and enjoy.

Nutritional Value (Amount per Serving):

- Calories 224
- Fat 8.9 g
- Carbohydrates 33.7 g
- Sugar 16.1 g
- Protein 3.7 g
- Cholesterol 48 mg

Baked Apple Slices

Preparation Time: 10 minutes

Cooking Time: 30 minutes

Serve: 6

Ingredients:

- 2 apples, peel, core, and slice
- 1 tsp cinnamon
- 2 tbsp butter
- 1/4 cup sugar
- 1/4 cup brown sugar
- 1/4 tsp salt

Directions:

1. Grease 9-inch round baking dish with cooking spray and set aside.
2. Add cinnamon, sugar, brown sugar, and salt into the zip-lock bag and mix well.
3. Add apple slices into the bag and shake until well coated.
4. Add apple slices into the prepared baking dish.
5. Select bake mode and set the omni to 350 F for 30 minutes once the oven beeps, place the baking dish into the oven.
6. Serve and enjoy.

Nutritional Value (Amount per Serving):

- Calories 128
- Fat 4 g
- Carbohydrates 24.8 g
- Sugar 21.9 g
- Protein 0.3 g
- Cholesterol 10 mg

Easy Blueberry Cake

Preparation Time: 10 minutes

Cooking Time: 45 minutes

Serve: 8

Ingredients:

- 1 egg
- 2 cups blueberries
- 1/2 cup butter, melted
- 2 cups all-purpose flour
- 1/2 cup milk
- 2 tsp baking powder
- 1/3 cup sugar
- Pinch of salt

Directions:

1. Grease 8-inch baking dish and set aside.
2. In a large bowl, mix together all-purpose flour, baking powder, sugar, and salt.
3. In a separate bowl, whisk egg, butter, and milk.
4. Add flour mixture into the egg mixture and mix until combined.
5. Pour batter into the prepared baking dish. Spread blueberries on top.
6. Select bake mode and set the omni to 350 F for 45 minutes once the oven beeps, place the baking dish into the oven.
7. Serve and enjoy.

Nutritional Value (Amount per Serving):

- Calories 284
- Fat 12.8 g
- Carbohydrates 38.8 g
- Sugar 12.8 g
- Protein 4.8 g
- Cholesterol 52 mg

Moist French Yogurt Cake

Preparation Time: 10 minutes

Cooking Time: 35 minutes

Serve: 12

Ingredients:

- 2 eggs
- 4 tbsp oil
- 7 oz sugar
- 7 oz all-purpose flour
- 2 tsp baking powder
- 8.5 oz yogurt

Directions:

1. In a large bowl, add yogurt, oil, eggs, sugar, flour, and baking powder and mix until smooth.
2. Pour batter into the greased cake pan.
3. Select bake mode and set the toaster oven to 350 F for 35 minutes once the oven beeps, place the cake pan into the oven.
4. Slice and serve.

Nutritional Value (Amount per Serving):

- Calories 188
- Fat 5.7 g
- Carbohydrates 31 g
- Sugar 18.1 g
- Protein 3.8 g
- Cholesterol 28 mg

Cinnamon Cranberry Muffins

Preparation Time: 10 minutes

Cooking Time: 30 minutes

Serve: 6

Ingredients:

- 2 eggs
- 1/2 cup cranberries
- 1/4 tsp cinnamon
- 1 tsp vanilla
- 1/4 cup sour cream
- 1 tsp baking powder
- 1/4 cup Swerve
- 1 1/2 cups almond flour
- Pinch of salt

Directions:

1. Line muffin tray with cupcake liners and set aside.
2. In a bowl, beat sour cream, vanilla, and eggs.
3. Add remaining ingredients except for cranberries and beat until smooth.
4. Add cranberries and fold well. Pour batter into the prepared muffin tray.
5. Select bake mode and set the omni to 325 F for 30 minutes once the oven beeps, place muffin tray into the oven.
6. Serve and enjoy.

Nutritional Value (Amount per Serving):

- Calories 90
- Fat 7 g
- Carbohydrates 3.5 g
- Sugar 0.8 g
- Protein 3.7 g
- Cholesterol 59 mg

Lemon Muffins

Preparation Time: 10 minutes

Cooking Time: 20 minutes

Serve: 12

Ingredients:

- 1 egg
- 1 cup ricotta cheese
- 1 tsp lemon extract
- 1 tbsp fresh lemon juice
- 1 tbsp lemon zest, grated
- 1/2 cup butter, softened
- 1 cup of sugar
- 1/2 tsp baking soda
- 1/2 tsp baking powder
- 2 cups flour
- 1/2 tsp salt

Directions:

1. Line muffin tray with cupcake liners and set aside.
2. In a mixing bowl, mix together egg, sugar, and butter.
3. Add lemon extract, lemon juice, lemon zest, and ricotta cheese and mix well.
4. In a separate bowl, mix together flour, baking soda, baking powder, and salt.
5. Add flour mixture into the egg mixture and mix until well combined.
6. Pour batter into the prepared muffin tray.
7. Select bake mode and set the omni to 350 F for 20 minutes once the oven beeps, place muffin tray into the oven.
8. Serve and enjoy.

Nutritional Value (Amount per Serving):

- Calories 242
- Fat 9.9 g
- Carbohydrates 33.9 g
- Sugar 16.9 g
- Protein 5.1 g
- Cholesterol 40 mg

Delicious Strawberry Bars

Preparation Time: 10 minutes

Cooking Time: 30 minutes

Serve: 16

Ingredients:

- 3/4 cup strawberry preserves
- 1 tsp xanthan gum
- 3/4 cup brown sugar
- 1 cup rolled oats
- 1 cup flour, gluten-free
- 1 tsp vanilla
- 10 tbsp butter, melted
- 1 tsp baking soda
- 1/4 tsp salt

Directions:

1. Grease 8*8 baking dish and set aside.
2. In a large bowl, whisk together flour, baking soda, xanthan gum, brown sugar, rolled oats, and salt.
3. Add melted butter and vanilla in flour mixture and stir to combine.
4. Set aside 1/3 of the flour mixture. Transfer the remaining mixture to the prepared baking dish and press down with a spatula.
5. Spread strawberry preserves on top.
6. Spread remaining flour mixture over the strawberry layer.
7. Select bake mode and set the omni to 350 F for 30 minutes once the oven beeps, place the baking dish into the oven.
8. Slice and serve.

Nutritional Value (Amount per Serving):

- Calories 180
- Fat 7.6 g
- Carbohydrates 26.7 g
- Sugar 14 g
- Protein 1.7 g
- Cholesterol 19 mg

Almond Butter Banana Brownies

Preparation Time: 10 minutes

Cooking Time: 20 minutes

Serve: 4

Ingredients:

- 1 scoop protein powder
- 2 tbsp cocoa powder
- 1/2 cup almond butter
- 1 cup bananas

Directions:

1. Spray baking dish with cooking spray.
2. Add all ingredients into the blender and blend until smooth.
3. Pour batter into the prepared baking dish.
4. Select bake mode and set the omni to 350 F for 20 minutes once the oven beeps, place the baking dish into the oven.
5. Serve and enjoy.

Nutritional Value (Amount per Serving):

- Calories 82
- Fat 2.1 g
- Carbohydrates 11.4 g
- Sugar 5 g
- Protein 6.9 g
- Cholesterol 16 mg

Pumpkin Muffins

Preparation Time: 10 minutes

Cooking Time: 35 minutes

Serve: 12

Ingredients:

- 2 eggs
- 1/2 cup maple syrup
- 1 tsp pumpkin pie spice
- 1 tsp baking soda
- 2 cups all-purpose flour
- 1/2 cup chocolate chips
- 1 cup can pumpkin
- 1/2 cup olive oil
- 1/2 tsp salt

Directions:

1. Line muffin tray with cupcake liners and set aside.
2. In a large bowl, mix together flour, pumpkin pie spice, baking soda, and salt.
3. In a separate bowl, whisk together eggs, pumpkin puree, oil, and maple syrup.
4. Slowly add dry mixture to the wet mixture and mix well. Add chocolate chips and fold well.
5. Pour batter into the prepared muffin tray.
6. Select bake mode and set the omni to 350 F for 35 minutes once the oven beeps, place muffin tray into the oven.
7. Serve and enjoy.

Nutritional Value (Amount per Serving):

- Calories 237
- Fat 11.5 g
- Carbohydrates 30.7 g
- Sugar 12.2 g
- Protein 3.8 g
- Cholesterol 29 mg

Conclusion

From healthy breakfast to delicious dinner and exquisite desserts, the Mediterranean Instant Omni Pro Air Fryer Oven Combo Cookbook has a great potential to be your new kitchen helper. This cookbook is a perfect start-up tool for beginners with no previous cooking experience, as long as for already experienced cooks who want to improve their knowledge and expand their cooking assortment.

What are you waiting for? Scroll up, click on "Buy Now" and start cooking the delicious and easy meals!

www.ingramcontent.com/pod-product-compliance
Lightning Source LLC
LaVergne TN
LVHW080921040225
802873LV00012B/191
* 9 7 8 1 9 1 5 0 3 8 3 8 8 *